Revised Edition

Herbal Cure

For Common & Chronic Diseases

AF556328

Dr. Aziz Ahmad Syed
Dr. Shiv Charan Sharma

PUSTAK MAHAL®

J-3/16 , Daryaganj, New Delhi-110002
☎ 23276539, 23272783, 23272784 • *Fax:* 011-23260518
E-mail: info@pustakmahal.com • *Website:* www.pustakmahal.com

Sales Centre
10-B, Netaji Subhash Marg, Daryaganj, New Delhi-110002
☎ 23268292, 23268293, 23279900 • *Fax:* 011-23280567
E-mail: rapidexdelhi@indiatimes.com

Branch Offices
Bengaluru: ☎ 22234025 • *Telefax:* 22240209
E-mail: pustak@airtelmail.in • pustak@sancharnet.in
Mumbai: ☎ 22010941
E-mail: rapidex@bom5.vsnl.net.in
Patna: ☎ 3294193 • *Telefax:* 0612-2302719
E-mail: rapidexptn@rediffmail.com
Hyderabad: *Telefax:* 040-24737290
E-mail: pustakmahalhyd@yahoo.co.in

© Pustak Mahal, Delhi

ISBN 978-81-223-0653-8

Edition: 2011

The Copyright of this book, as well as all matter contained herein (including illustrations) rests with the Publishers. No person shall copy the name of the book, its title design, matter and illustrations in any form and in any language, totally or partially or in any distorted form. Anybody doing so shall face legal action and will be responsible for damages.

Printed at : **Param Offsetters, Okhla, Delhi**

Dedication

This book is dedicated

to my father to whom

Ayurvedic/Unani medicines

have given new lease of life.

—Dr. S. Aziz Ahmad

Acknowledgement

I am thankful to Mr. Abhinav Saxena, M.Sc., my student who came up to me with your advertisement of book writing on Herbal Drugs, Prof. M.S. Usmani, for his valuable suggestions and discussions, Mr. R.C. Sharma, Typist and Krishna Studio for photography.

Courtesies:

1. Photographs (Medicinal Plants/R. Chief and Heal with Herbs/S. Dahanukar).
2. Literatures (Baidyanath and Hamdard)

— Dr. S. Aziz Ahmad
— Dr. Shiv Charan Sharma

Preface

"The oldest existing health care, a heritage of ancient India. While the written records of this system of natural health care date back to almost 5000 years, it has of late also been recognised by the W.H.O. as an effective complementary health system."

Phyto-therapy—a kind of treatment with plants and herbs (commonly referred to as Ayurveda/Unani system of medicines) far from abandoned is enjoying revival. The plant as a whole is considered to be more efficacious than the separate substances. Its slow curative or healing property is due to low concentration of chemicals present in it or probably due to synergic.

Several UNESCO backed scientific projects studying grandmother cures are going on all over the world. Even the SAARC countries are mooted to make an exhaustive inventory of all medicinal plants in the region.

Ayurvedic products are now incorporated in the U.S.A. There is also a formation of a medical council whose role is to create authentic herbal formulae based on the Ayurvedic/ Unani texts.

About 30% ingredients of all allopathic medicines and 100% of Ayurvedic, Unani and homeopathy medicines come from plants.

As evident from the present scenario, herbal cure is getting worldwide acceptance and thus emphasising modern scientific evaluation/extraction of medicines from plants/folk medicines.

—Authors

Contents

1. Diabetes 9
2. Liver and related diseases : Hepato-biliary dysfunctions 21
3. Blood Pressure/Heart Disease Hypertension/Heart Problems 30
4. Gastro-Intestinal Disorders 40
5. Intestinal Worms and Related Diseases 51
6. Urinary Diseases 57
7. Management of Cancer : Herbal Approaches 66
8. Plant Foods and their Nutritive Values 76
9. Disturbed Menses and Related Problems 89
10. Mental Diseases 97
11. Skin Diseases 107
12. Rheumatic Diseases 115
13. (a) Plant Drugs Prepared by Allopathic Drug Companies 122
13. (b) Comparative Study of Herbal Preparations of Baidyanath and Hamdard 125
13. (c) Herbal Tips 133
14. Miracles of Water Therapy 148
15. Some Herbal Preparations of Himalaya Drug Company 150

Glossary 156

Bibliography 165

1
Diabetes

Diabetes mellitus (madhumeha) was known to ancient Indian physicians 3000 years ago. An elaborate description of its clinical features and its effective management has been discussed in Ayurvedic texts. It was stated in the Ayurveda that insects and flies were attracted to the urine of some people, which tasted sweet. The ancient Indian sage Sushruta in 1000 B.C. diagnosed diabetes.

Diabetes is a disease in which the body does not produce enough insulin or does not use insulin properly to convert food into energy. The term diabetes mellitus derives from the Greek—diabainess to pass through and the Latin mellitus 'sweetened with honey'.

The body derives most of its energy from sugars, starches and other foods. The hormone insulin is responsible for converting these chemicals into energy. Insulin is secreted by the pancreas, a gland near the stomach. Without the action of insulin, sugar piles up in the blood stream (hyperglycemia) and spills into the urine (glycosurea) while the other tissues starve. Microscopic blood vessels are slowly damaged leading to early cataract formation, even to blindness and kidney damage. Nerves are disrupted causing pain and numbness in the extremities. Besides, it is causing problem to heart, it also gradually develops into a syndrome.

There are almost 100 million people suffering from diabetes worldwide but today because of advances in medicine, diabetics can look forward to a normal life with an excellent quality of life. There are two main types of diabetes: Diabetes insipedius and Diabetes mellitus.

Diabetes insipedius

An uncommon disorder in which excess urine is formed due to failure of the pituitary gland's hormonal secretion antidiuretic hormone (ADH). The primary defect may be in the pituitary gland itself or in the hypothalamus, the part of the brain floor that controls secretion of the hormone. This defect is corrected by giving ADH by injection or snuff or nasal drops.

Diabetes mellitus

Diabetes mellitus or simply diabetes, is the result of a deficiency of insulin. The deficiency can be caused in more than one way, so that diabetes is a group of diseases with similar symptoms, not a single disease.

Deficiency of insulin may be absolute, when the pancreas does not form a normal amount or it may be relative, when the patient does not use insulin properly and needs more than even a normal pancreas can secrete. A man whose pancreas has been removed secretes no insulin at all. He needs injections of 20-30 units of insulin daily to remain healthy. Many diabetics form much more insulin than this for themselves, yet need a larger daily injection than people with no pancreas—because they have antagonists to insulin in their tissues and most of the insulin is wasted, or because their body cells (particularly those of the liver) do not respond normally to insulin. However the exact nature of the antagonism to insulin is not known. Several hormones from (pituitary, adrenal, thyroid, and glucagon from pancreas itself) oppose the action of insulin, and a few cases of diabetes can be blamed on an excess of one of them—e.g., diabetes as a symptom of cushing's syndrome, which is an excess of adrenal hormones. In most cases, antibodies which combine with insulin and neutralize it may be the cause, or it may be that the liver takes up insulin and arrests it, which has the same effect.

Effect of diabetes

Glucose should be released from the liver into the blood and taken up by cells throughout the body to be oxidised (burnt) to carbon dioxide and water. In some way insulin enables glucose to pass through the outer membrane of cell. If there is no insulin, glucose is not taken up but accumulates in blood.

The effects are far reaching. The most obvious and least important are: excess of glucose in blood (which is quite harmless), overflow of glucose into urine, and increased volume of urine to carry the glucose. Increased volume of urine causes severe thirst. As mentioned below it is one of the symptoms of diabetes.

The secondary effects in body chemistry are more significant. Because glucose can not be burnt, fat is burnt instead, and the patient loses weight. But the combustion of fat can be completed i.e., brought to the end products carbon dioxide and water, only in the presence of reagents formed during the combustion of glucose. Since glucose is not being burnt, fat combustion stops half-way. The intermediate products—ketone bodies collect in sufficient amount to become poisonous. This causes severe acidosis and finally coma, in which the patient is likely to die unless given insulin. As well as fat, protein is consumed as fuel, so that muscle and other tissues are weakened.

Another factor due to diabetes is the degeneration of small blood vessels of eyes and kidneys. These organs are more prone to the effect and uncontrolled diabetes can lead to defective vision or even blindness, and a form of bright's disease of the kidneys (a disease of the kidney of toxic origin, affecting the glomeruli, tubules, and intestinal tissue in varying degree). The nerves of the limbs are sometimes effected by diabetic neuritis (neuropathy), with tingling, numbness and other troubles; this may be due to interference with their blood supply.

Diabetics are also susceptible to disease of large arteries

(Fatty degeneration of the arterial wall) with its complications such as angina. This may be due to disturbed fat chemistry.

Another common complication is bacterial infection. A crop of boils is often seen.

Symptoms

- Increased urination
- Excessive thirst
- Loss of weight with normal diet
- Sugar (glucose) in urine
- Degeneration of small blood vessels of eyes
- Kidney dysfunctions

Causes

- Over weight
- Sedentary life
- Excess sweets and overeating
- Rich food
- Hereditary
- Lack of physical activities

Treatment

People used to die young until 1921, when Banting and Best isolated fairly pure insulin solving the problem of diabetes treatment. But insulin is no cure, because the patient needs daily injections for the rest of his life. To be sure, a dose of insulin is no more a permanent cure of diabetes than a drink of water is a permanent cure of thirst; but while the effect lasts the cure is complete and the patient is in all respects healthy.

After insulin many synthetic e.g., tolbutamide, phenorformin etc. are prepared but have temporary effects and also not free from side reactions. So, plants were tried and found useful and cheap in controlling the diabetes and that too without any side effects.

Overall treatment is based on the following points:

- Avoid sugar, fat and starchy food material.
- The food habits should be regulated after urine examination (normal blood sugar level is 80-120 mg/ 100 cc of blood).
- Weight should be gradually reduced if over-weight.
- Regular use of anti-diabetic drugs.

Tips

- Long morning walk is essential.
- Avoid injuries because healing is slow in diabetics.
- Take wholesome granular food items: *Chana, Jau, Pulses* etc.
- Restrict day sleep, rather avoid it.
- Eat light foods, that too in small shifts.

Role of Plants

1. Momordica charantia, Linn.

Family	— Cucurbitaceae		
Names	— Hindi	— Karela	
	English	— Bitter Gourd	
	Sanskrit	— Karavella	
	Bengali	— Karela	
	Marathi	— Karle	
	Kannada	— Hagal	
	Tamil	— Pakal, Pavakka	
	Malayalam	— Kaippakaya	

Description: It is a climber, stem is slender pubescent with suborbicular leaves and single pale flowers. Fruits are 5-25 cm long, pendulous, fusiform, beaked and ribbed with many tubercles. Brown seed, 13-16 cm long compressed in bulb of fruit.

Distribution: Plant is cultivated during hot season and available in Indian market as vegetable.

Parts used: Roots, leaves and fruits.

Phytochemicals: Different types of compounds have been isolated viz., bitter glycosides, saponins, alkaloids, reducing sugars, phenolics, oils, free acids, polypeptides, sterols, 17-amino acids including methionine and a crystalline products named p-insulin.

Vitamins — B_1, B_2 and C
Minerals — Calcium, phosphorous, iron, copper and potassium.

Properties

Hypoglycemic (reducing sugar in the blood), astringent (arresting secretion), anti-haemorrhoidal (tending to arrest or prevent bleeding), stomachic (promoting digestion improve appetite), emmenagogue (inducing menstruation), galactogogue (increase the secretion or flow of milk), hepatic stimulant, anthelmintic (power to destroy worms) and blood purifier.

Forms of use: In form or juice, decoction (in liquid form after boiling), and powder.

Medicinal uses

(a) In Diabetes

Bitter gourd (Karela) is the most efficient drug found to be effective in controlling the blood sugar. A lot of work has been done to study hypoglycemic and anti-diabetic activity of Karela. Its root leaves and fruit extracts are used as folk remedy for diabetes mellitus from ancient times and proved to be powerful hypoglycemic agents. It is used in the various forms as written below:

i. 100 gm. of fresh Karela powder in a divided dose two times for 2 weeks bring down sugar level considerably.

ii. Juice of its leaves or concentrated extract has same hypoglycemic properties like tolbutamide. So juice of Karela two tablespoonfuls two times for a month controls diabetes.

iii. A mixture of Jamun, Gurmar, Neem and Karela (leaves only) in the ratio 2:1:1:2 is found to be effective remedy for diabetes.

(b) Other uses

The roots are used as astringent and in piles. The fruits are stomachic and also used in gout, rheumatism and in liver and spleen diseases. Fruit juice with sugar used in stomatitis (inflammation of the mucous membrane of the mouth) and as an emmenagogue in dysmenorrhoea (pain occurring in the back and lower abdomen at or about the time of the menses).

The juice of leaves is used as an *emetic* (producing vomiting), *purgative* (promotes evacuation of the bowel) *in bilious affections* and also in relieving burning of the soles of the feet. The fruits and leaves are used as anthelmintic and also in piles, jaundice and as vermifuge (any substance which causes the expulsion of parasitic worms). Leaves act as a galactogogue (secretion of milk). The leaf juice with black pepper is applied locally for night blindness. The fruit juice given for 3 days (25 ml) once in the morning is said to exert contraceptive effect.

Doses—Juice 10-15 ml, Powder 2-5 g.

2. Pterocarpus marsupium, Roxb

Family — Fabaceae

Names — Hindi — Vijaisar kaashtha

English — Indian kinowood

Sanskrit — *Piṭasala* Asana, Peetasaar, Sarfaka

Telugu — Paiddagi Chekka

Marathi — Biyala lakda

Tamil — Vegaimaram chakkal

Trade name — Bijaisaar Kaashtha

Description: A moderate to large tree about 90 ft or more high. Leaves compound, having 5-7 leaflets, 3 to 5 inch long, oblong or elliptic, margin wavy, flower about 1.5 cm long, yellow in colour.

The heartwood of this tree is golden yellow. Tree bark yields a reddish gum called kino, the trade name.

Distribution: The tree is common in central and peninsular India, found at 3000 ft in Gujarat, Madhya Pradesh and Sub-Himalayan Tract. Also available in Indian Market.

Phytochemicals: Glycosides, flavours, terpenes, phenols.

Parts used: Bark, gum, flowers, leaves, heartwood.

Properties

Astringent, alterant (A drug which corrects, or is presumed to correct disordered bodily function), hypoglycemic.

Medicinal Uses

(a) In Diabetes

1. The tree has been regarded as useful in diabetes from ancient time. The water, in which a block of wood of this tree has been soaked overnight is given to diabetic patients.
2. Water stored overnight in a tumbler made of this wood has shown anti-diabetic properties. People often seen using such tumbler for drinking water.
3. Decoction of bark 56 to 112 ml once in the morning for 10-15 days is useful in controlling diabetes.
4. Powdered bark 3 to 6 g or extracted juice 125 mg 2/3 times after meals control diabetes.
5. Powdered bark 5 g left overnight in a cup of water. Next day, water is decanted and taken on empty stomach in the morning for 10 days checks diabetes. Promising results have been reported with regard to reduction in the sugar levels in blood and urine.

(b) Other Uses

The gum (Kino) which is obtained from incisions in bark is astringent (a substance that shrinks soft tissues and contracts blood vessels thus checking the flow of blood) and used in leucoderma, diarrhoea, pyrosis (heart burn; gastric hyperacidity) and toothache. Bruised leaves are used externally for boils, sores and various skin diseases. It promotes the complexion of the skin. The flowers are used in fevers. The plant is considered to be useful by santhal tribals in burns, syphilis, stomachache, cholera, dysentery and menorrhagia (Excessive or prolonged periods).

Doses

Decoction	—	50 to 100 ml
Powder	—	3 to 6 g
Extracted Juice	—	125 mg

3. Syzygium cumini, (Linn) Skeels

Family	:	Myrtaceae	
Names	:	Hindi	— Jamun
		English	— Black berry
		Sanskrit	— Jambul
		Bengali	— Kalijaam bija
		Kannada	— Koddanirlu kalu
		Marathi	— Jambhul chabi
		Gujarati	— Jambunu bija
		Tamil	— Sambal virat
		Telugu	— Naredu vittulu
		Trade name	— Jambul stone

Description: A large evergreen tree, leaves opposite, 8-20cm long, leathery. Fruit 1.5-4 cm long, violet black on ripe. Seed usually one. Fruits are eaten raw with salt, make tongue purple for hours.

Distribution: Grown throughout the plains of India.

Parts used: Fruits, leaves, seeds and bark.

Properties: Astingent, stomachic, diuretic (increases the amount of urine), anti-diabetic and anti-diarrhoeal.

Phytochemicals: Phenols, terpenes, glucoside.

Medicinal Uses

(a) In diabetes

1. The seeds are useful in diabetes. The fruit juice also has this property but the effect of preparations from seeds is more marked.
2. Aqueous extract of seeds produced marked fall in blood sugar in a single dose.
3. Jamun's vinegar is also useful in controlling diabetes. Regular use is recommended with both the meals.
4. Use of mixture prepared by mixing dried fruit of Karela (10g), Pterocarpus bark (10g) and Jamun seed (10g). After proper grinding take water extract of 2/3g of this powder to keep diabetes at bay.

(b) Other Uses

The bark is astringent and used in sore throats, indigestion, loss of appetite, leucorrhoea (A discharge of white from uterus and the vagina), bronchitis, asthma, ulcers and dysentry; it is also given for purifying blood, and as gargle for spongy gum. The fresh juice of bark with goat's milk is given in diarrhoea. Ripe fruit can also check diarrhoea.

Doses

Juice	—	50 to 100 ml
Bark Powder	—	0.5 to 1.0 g
Seeds	—	1.0 to 3.0 g

Other Useful Plants

- *Azadirachta indica* **(Neem)** extract also has marked hypoglycemic properties.
- *Gymnema sylvestre* **(Gurmar)** Leaf material stimulates insulin secretion and has blood sugar reducing properties.
- *Tenospora cordifolia* **(Gilo)** enhances glucose utilization and checks release of glucose from the liver.
- *Casearia esculenta* **(Chilla)** increases the utilization of

glucose by the body.

- *Ficus bengalensis* **(Bargad)** sap of this tree is effective in controlling the diabetes and increasing capacity of pancreatic cells.
- *Coccinia indica* **(Bimbi)** plant reduces blood sugar.
- *Helicterus isora* **(Mororphali)** decoction or juice of root bark given in diabetes to lessen the quantity of sugar.
- *Catharanthus roseus* **(Sadabahar, Violet Flowers)** also possesses hypoglycemic properties. Five leaves three times a day keeps diabetes in control.
- *Luffa acutangula* **(Turai)** is also useful in diabetes as it reduces the level of sugar.
- *Lawsonia inermis* **(Mehndi)**. The seed extract is a proven remedy for diabetes.

Plants helping the diabetics indirectly (because diabetes may lead to the conditions like hyper-lipidaemia, arthosclerosis and mycordial infraction etc.) are *Trichosanthus dioca* (Parval), *Gyamposes tetragoloba* (Juar) *Plumago zeylanica* (Chitrak), *Boswellia serrata* (Bhilawan) and *Commiphora mukal* (Gum Guggul) which lowers down the total cholesterol when taken over a period of time.

Diabetes that starts in middle age is generally a much milder disease. The patient is commonly overweight when first symptoms appear. Overeating brings diseases like obesity, diabetes, hyper-lipidaemia, arthosclerosis, coronary heart disease and other maladies. Diabetes is incurable but a managable disease, often strikes late in one's life. The reason behind it is the limited supply of effective insulin. By eating less one can keep well because his diet will remain within the limit of what his own insulin can manage.

Diabetes can only be controlled by adopting an optimistic view on life and by following a good diet regimen and exercise.

As it is rightly said, "When people tell you diabetes

cannot be controlled, ask them to go and take a walk". Even the simplest form of exercise, like walking helps to control diabetes. Exercise improves metabolism which in turn leads to better control of glucose. It also helps to reduce weight and lowers blood pressure—which is commonly elevated in diabetics. More importantly, exercise can facilitate reduction of insulin dosage and other oral drugs. Along with regular exercise you must also control your diet. And remember to substitute your sugar with aspartame-based sweetners. So, control the urge to take a cab for short distances. Walk instead. You could be walking away from diabetes.

Medicines

Ayurvedic	—	Madhumeha
Unani	—	Dolabı
Homeopathic	—	Uranium drops, 5-10 drops in half cup water 3 times daily.

2

Liver and related diseases: Hepato-biliary dysfunctions

The liver, the body's central chemical laboratory and its most important detoxicator, has over 500 functions to carry out. Its chief function is to provide bile for digestion but besides this it acts as a master chemist, supplier, housekeeper and controller.

The liver is the largest, heaviest and the most solid organ in the body. A tough gland, one of its functions is to rebuild and regenerate cells. Sometimes, in case of liver cancer, 90 percent of the liver is removed but it is able to function and grow back to its original size.

The liver is the most important organ of the body. A storage house, it holds fats, sugars and proteins that come from the digestive tract. The liver makes this food available to the cells in the form that is required. It produces the fat like substances iecithin and cholesterol and bile which is necessary for the digestion of fats and the absorption of vitamins A, D, E and K. It not only stores these vitamins but also minerals like iron, copper, trace elements required for the body.

The liver, with the help of insulin, regulates sugar according to the needs of the body. It also detoxifies harmful substances that may damage the cell. Nitrogen-containing waste products from worn-out cell proteins are broken down and antibodies to destroy bacteria are produced. In short, the liver acts as a defence against disease.

Diseases occur when the acidic content of the body

increases. The body constantly strives to maintain a slightly alkaline medium (blood) and when the acidic content of the blood increases, the liver—which is the largest storehouse of the alkaline mineral sodium—releases sodium quickly into the bloodstream to maintain the balance. Diseases occur when this function of the liver is undermined due to wrong living habits which lead to a rise in acidity. When the liver is depleted of sodium, illness results. In fact if the liver could keep the bloodstream clean by filtering out damaging poisons, we would have lived indefinitely.

When the liver is healthy and vital, it carries out functions smoothly, giving good health; but in the process it loses its own vitality, resulting in a disease, crisis and becoming more toxic.

Hepato-biliary system includes liver, gall bladder, spleen and pancreas. A deep investigation into the history of malfunctioning of these organs revealed that the root cause is commonly what is known as sluggish hepatic activity. An earlier attack and after effects of jaundice, malaria, influenza, typhoids, dysentery, besides gallstone cholecystitis (inflammation of the gall bladder), pancreatitis (inflammation of pancreas), enlargement of spleen, liver and treatment thereof, may be the major cause leading to sluggish hepatic functions. These organs are interconnected so malfunctioning of anyone affects all the organs specially liver.

Allopathic system of treatment though much advanced one is yet to provide some dependable synthetic preparation to correct hepato-biliary dysfunctions. It is only preparation from medicinal plants that comes to rescue whenever such problem arises. The medicinal plants mostly bitter are indicated in hepatic insufficiency, intestinal putrefaction and irregular bile flow, habitual biliousness, chronic dyspepsia (difficulty in digestion), chronic cholecystitis, intestinal auto intoxication, jaundice, early cirrhosis (degeneration of liver), hepatitis, fat intolerance, fatty infilteration of liver and allied troubles.

The plants described help to stimultate the hepatic cells,

producing abundant flow of bile, normalise gastrointestinal inactivity in general and are beneficial in various hepato-biliary dysfunctions. They correct torpidity of the liver, stimulate separation in the stomach and intestine, cure habitual biliousness, chronic dyspepsia, jaundice and cirrhosis. A prolonged use of these plants revitalizes the liver cells by virtue of their compounds present in them which drain out heavy toxins deposition by working as solvent for such pigments and combined effects of *Cassia augustifolia* and *Foeniculum vulgare* give it a fine cholagogue (promoting the flow of bile) action and regeneration hepatic functions in all aspects and thereby increasing duodenal digestion, appetite and removing constipation etc. Few plants which deserve special attention in this regards are *Phylanthus niruri, Picrorhiza kurroa, Capparis spinosa, Andrographis paniculata,* and *Fumaria officinallis.* These plants in combination with other drugs is a quick and effective cure for catarrhal jaundice, enlargement of liver and gall bladder. They prevent post hepatic syndrome, can be given in post therapy stage of jaundice to restore normal functional phenomenon after organic treatment is over but not as a sole therapeutic agent for the treatment of catarrhal jaundice, and in advance cases of cirrhosis.

In case of poor assimilation power, a course of these plants' extract given 2-3 week prior to a tonic served as an anabolic agent, enhancing the results from the tonic during convalescene. Thus, it helps in rundown stage to gain speedy recovery, continuous use of these plants improves digestion and aids movements of bowels and helps to set right the entire digestive system. They also protect, as said from viral-hepatitis, toxic hepatitis including drug induced hepatitis and alcoholic hepatitis, chronic cholecystitis and promoting appetite plus growth.

Symptoms

- Loss of appetite and weight.
- Feeling of nausea.
- Feeling of dizziness.

- Pain on the right side of stomach (Just below the ribs).
- Pain in the stomach pit.
- Yellowness of eyes.
- Feeling of unwell and indigestion.
- Excessive gas formation and gastric refluxes.

Role of Plants

1. Andrographis paniculata (Burm.f.) Wall.ex. Nees

Family	:	Acanthaceae		
Names	:	Hindi	–	Kaalmegha
		Sanskrit	–	Kalpanaatha
		English	–	The Creat
		Bengali	–	Kaalmegha
		Marathi	–	Olikiryata
		Gujarati	–	Lilu kriyaatu
		Tamil	–	Nilavendu
		Trade name	–	Kaalmegha

Description: An erect branched annual herb, branches sharply four angled. Leaves lance-shaped. Flowers small, in large, spreading and sparse bunches. Flowers rose-coloured, about 1 cm long. Fruit capsular, 1.5-2 cm.

Distribution: The plant occurs throughout India, chiefly in the plains.

Parts used: Whole herb.

Chemical compounds: Bitter principle, kalmeghin flavone, essential oil etc.

Properties: Root and leaves are stomachic, tonic, antipyretic (lower fever), alterant, anthelmentic, febrifuge (Any drug which mitigates or removes fever) and cholagogue.

Forms of Use: Tincture, poultice (a soft medicated and usually heated mass applied to the body and kept in place with muslin etc. for relieving soreness and inflammation), juice.

Medicinal Uses

It is reported to be a powerful drug for liver and allied complaints. Decoction or infusion of the leaves gives good results in sluggish liver. It is a major constituent of *Switraadi lepa,* an effective drug for Vitilago, Kaalmegha navayas churna and Kaalmegha aasava.

Other Uses

Kaalmegha is a bitter tonic, it is useful in curing fever, worms, dysentery, general weakness and excessive gas formation in stomach and indigestion. Tribals of Bastar (M.P) pound the plant in mustard oil and apply on itching.

Doses

Infusion 10-15 ml; functions 3-5 ml. Juice of leaves and stems 1 to 4 ml.

2. Phyllanthus niruri, ***Auct/non Linn.***

Family	:	Euphorbiaceae	
Names	:	Hindi	– Jar amla or Jangli amla
		Sanskrit	– Bhumyamlaki
		English	– Niruri
		Tamil	– Kizhkay neli
		Bengali	– Bhuinamla
		Kannada	– Kirunelli
		Trade name	– Bhuiaamla

Distribution: Throughout the northern parts of India.

Parts used: Whole herb.

Description: An annual weed 2ft high, leaves small, alternate, arranged in two rows, membranous, usually thin and glaucous under surface, elliplic, narrow at the base, stipules two. Flowers very small, monoecious, in pairs in the axils of leaves capsule, globose, slightly depressed at the top with six ridges.

Form of Use: Infusion, powder, juice, decoction (extraction of the essence of a substance by boiling in water).

Properties: Diuretic, astringent, cooling, laxative (helps in evacuation of bowel) and bitter tonic.

Chemical Compounds: Alkaloids, bitter, compounds, lignans, flavones.

Medicinal Uses

(a) Liver and related diseases

1. It is found to be effective in the treatment of infective hepatitis without any side effects. It is useful in all liver and related troubles viz., malfunctioning of spleen, gall bladder, liver and pancreas to the extent that it is found to be hypoglycemic. It provides solo cure for jaundice and no other plant is needed.
2. The fresh root is given in jaundice and aqueous extract of leaves inactivate the hepatitis B.
3. A dosage of 50 mg/kg in 3 divided daily dosage has been claimed to be effective in the treatment of infective hepatitis. In majority of cases while disappearance of (1) jaundice hepatitis of tenderness and (2) bile salts and pigments from urine is observed after a week. It takes two weeks more to clear almost all the symptoms following improvement in general condition and appetite.
4. The juice of P. niruri is famous remedy for all types of jaundice.

(b) Other Uses

Decoction of the herb is given for dropsical disorders, gonorrhoea (an inflammatory disease of the genito-urinary passage), constipation, stomach ache, dyspepsia (difficulty in digestion) and dysentery. The juice of the plant is an efficacious dressing for offensive sores, mixed with some bland oil, the juice is used in ophthalmia (conjunctivitis or inflammation of eyes). The young leaves are useful in the milder forms of intermittent fevers; boiled in milk, they are given in dropsical disorders and urinary complaints.

A poultice of the leaves made with rice water is applied to ulcers or edematous swelling and is used for the treatment of itch and scabies and other skin diseases. The fresh roots with rice water is given in menorrhagia (excessively profuse discharge of the menses, or their excessive prolongation) and in galactagogue (producing milk or increasing the secretion of it).

Doses

Infusion 10-20 ml.
Powder 1 to 2 g.

3. Picrorhiza kurroa, Roxle ex Benth.

Family	:	Scrophul ariaceae		
Names	:	Hindi	–	Kutu kasohini
		Sanskrit	–	Katula
		English	–	Picrohiza root
		Bengali	–	Kataki
		Gujarati	–	Kadu
		Marathi	–	Kutaki
		Trade name	–	Karu; Kutari

Description: The herb is more or less hairy, with perennial woody, bitter rhizome 15 to 25 cm long clothed with dry leaf bases. Leaves spathulate serrate, 5 to 10 cm long, rather coriaceous with rounded tips, and the base is narrowed into winged sheathing petioles. Flowers small, in spikes, bracteate bracts-oblong or lanceolate, as long as the calyx. Sepals 5, lanceolate 6mm long, ciliate, flowers dimorphic. They are of two kinds: Some have a 8mm long filament, others have 2 cm long filaments. Fruits 1 to 3 cm long. The rhizomes of the plant are cylindrical with an average diameter of 2 cm.

Distribution: A perennial herb, found in alpine Himalayas from Kashmir to Sikkim at altitudes of 9000-12000 ft.

Parts used: Dried rhizome.

Properties: Stomachic, laxative, cathartic (having a

purging or relating to purgation), antiperiodic (acting against the periodic recurrence of a disease) i.e. antimalarial, cholagogue (promoting the flow of bile).

Chemical Compounds: Flavone, saponin, alkaloids, sterols.

Medicinal Uses

(a) Liver and related diseases

The root is also used in diseases of liver and spleen including jaundice and anaemia.

Its solo preparation picrolive alone works wonder for liver dysfunction and allied diseases.

In clinical studies on patients of infective hepatitis with jaundice, *P. Kurroe* was reported to have led to a rapid fall in serum bilirubin (a deep yellow coloured compound whose formation increases in jaundice) levels toward normal range and quicker clinical recovery with no side effects.

A more potent preparation may work in better way if all three plants *A. paniculate, P. niruri* and *P. kurroae* are mixed together as herbal cure for all hepato-biliary dysfunctions.

(b) Other Uses

A study claimed that *P. kurroa* led to beneficial results in the management of bronchial asthma. The drug is also reported to produce marked reduction of serum cholesterol and coagulation time. Roots are used in dyspepsia and fever.

Dose

Powder as a tonic—1 to 1.5 g.

Other Useful Plants

- *Boerhavia diffusa* **(Punarnava).** Increases the liver ATP phosphodrolase activity and is useful in jaundice and inflammatory conditions.
- *Capparis spinosa* **(Kabra).** Very useful as a biliary

deobstructive, in liver disorder and enlarged spleen.

- *Cassia augustifolia* **(Sanai).** It is also a liver stimulant and powerful laxative.
- *Cinchorium intybus* **(Kasni).** Useful in liver, spleen enlargement and gall ailments.
- *Emblica officinallis* **(Amla).** It has cooling effect on liver and is effective in jaundice.
- *Foeniculum vulgare* **(Soya).** Useful in spleen trouble.
- *Fumaria officinalis* **(Pitpapra).** Stops wandering of mind, good for the diseases of spleen, dyspepsia due to torpor of the liver.
- *Solanum nigrum* **(Makoi).** Helpful in correcting acute and chronic enlargement of liver and useful in the cirrhosis.
- *Swertia chirata* **(Chiraita).** Useful in liver trouble and allied complaints.
- *Taraxacum officinala* **(Kanphool).** Has a specific action on cholecystitis (inflammation of the gall bladder) and is thought to have a lithontriptic action on hepatic calculi. It also increases the flow of bile.
- *Tephrosia purpurea* **(Surphonka).** Useful in disorder of spleen and liver.
- *Terminalia chebula* **(Harr).** Is also recommended in spleen and liver disorders.

People with torpid liver or sluggish biliary function are sometimes advised to undergo a special cure based on eating grapes. As it is understood that some ailments of liver can be corrected easily by taking sugar/glucose i.e. by drinking a glass of sharbat or two daily.

Medicines

Ayurvedic — Liv-52, Stimuliv, Eladi Churna
Unani — Jawarish Amla, Kushta Jamrud, Kushta Faulad
Homeopathic — Livotex, Chelidonium-30, 3 times daily.

3

Blood Pressure/Heart Disease Hypertension/Heart problems

The heart is a vital organ of our body which pumps the blood to all the systems through the arteries of the body. The blood is passed through arterial vessels which are elastic in nature. Blood pressure is nothing but the pressure exerted by it on the vessels' walls. There are two types of blood pressure: Systolic and diastolic. Systolic blood pressure is that pressure which is exerted by the blood on the walls of the arteries during contractive phase of the heart, diastolic blood pressure is that pressure which is exerted by the blood on its vessel walls during the expansive phase. Normally the blood pressure increases during emotion, excitement and anger and is low during sleep and rest. It varies from person to person with age, sex, mental and physical work of the individual. Hypertension may be due to the thickening of the arterial wall (Arterio-sclerosis) especially in old age or it may be due to stress and strain. Disorder of kidney may also produce hypertension.

Symptoms

- Heaviness, oppression, discomfort or chest pain which may be localised or radiate to the left arm.
- Pain in chest intensifies on exertion or after meals.
- Recent undue breathlessness after climbing two flights of stairs.
- Sudden fatigue after exercise.
- Palpitation or rapid heart beats or irregular heart beats.
- Sudden weakness or numbness in the upper or lower or

both extremities.

- Fainting or coma or loss of speech or slurring of words.
- Headache not relieved by aspirin or any common drug.
- Blurring of vision or hearing.
- Transient attacks of giddiness which come on when the head is suddenly turned to one side.

Causes

Exact cause is not known but mental exertion/worries, too much fat, overweight and excessive use of alcohol and salt may be the cause. A sudden fall can cause fainting and low perfusion-ichaemic injury to the heart tissues. Abrupt swings in blood pressure are dangerous as it can rupture vessels in the retina or brain or cause overburdened heart to fail. So, blood pressure above 150/90 and below 120/70 should not be left untreated and requires medical attention.

Treatment

It is based on strict regimen that includes control on diets, exercise and drugs/plants.

Role of Plants

1. Allium cepa, L

Family	—	Liliaceae		
Name	—	Hindi	—	Piyaz
		Sanskrit	—	Palandu
		English	—	Onion
		Bengali	—	Pyanj
		Marathi	—	Kanda
		Gujarati	—	Dungari
		Malayalam	—	Chuvannauli
		Kannada	—	Nirulli
		Tamil	—	Vengayam
		Telugu	—	Nirulli

Description: The bulbous root of this plant consists of layers of fleshy scales covered by white, yellow or violet coloured tunics. The erect stem is hollow with a swelling at the lower end and can grow as high as 2-3 ft. The hollow leaves, which are almost cylindrical or slightly flattened, have a smooth surface. The flowers, which have white or purple petals, are clustered into rounded heads. The fruit consists of one capsule and 3 loculi with flat, black seeds.

Distribution: Cultivated throughout India.

Parts used: Bulb.

Phytochemicals: Essential oil containing allylic disulphides, sugar, inulin, quercetin, calcium, biflavonoids.

Properties: Diuretic, antibiotic, hypoglycemic, hypotensive (lower blood pressure), anti-inflammatory, lithotripic (pertaining to removal of stone), anthelmintic, analgesic, anti-neuralgic, expectorant, anti-rheumatic and corn remover.

Forms of use : Decoction, fluid extract, tincture, poultice, ointment and juice.

Medicinal Uses

(a) In blood pressure

(i) One teaspoonful onion juice with honey should be taken for 15-20 days to bring down the blood pressure.

(ii) Regular use of raw onion especially its yellowish and purplish scales with meals help keeping blood pressure in control.

(iii) Raw onion juice with honey and ginger juice reduces blood pressure and cholesterol level.

(b) Other Uses

Onions have antiseptic value for the entire alimentary canal It is stimulant, diuretic and expectorant. Mixed with common salt, onion is a remedy for colic and scurvy and the roasted onion is applied as poultice to indolent boils and haemorrhoids (a venous swelling at the anus; a pile). Onion juice is often smelled for the recovery from faintness besides being used in infantile convulsions, headache, epileptic and hysterical fits.

A decoction of the onion is beneficial for checking extreme heat sensation. To relieve ear-ache warm onion juice is dropped in the ear.

2. Allium sativum, Linn.

Family	:	Liliaceae	
Names	:	Hindi	— Lahsun
		Sanskrit	— Rasana
		English	— Garlic
		Bengali	— Rasuna
		Tamil	— Vallaipunelu
		Gujarati	— Lasana
		Telugu	— Velluli
		Trade name	— Lahasuna

Description: It is well known, bulbous, herbaceous plant which grows to about 2-3 ft height. The bulb consists of 8-10 curved bulblets (cloves). The stem is erect and hollow.

Distribution: Cultivated throughout India.

Parts used: Bulb.

Phytochemicals: Alliin, allicin, inulin, essential oil.

Vitamins —A, B and C
Minerals —Selenium

Properties: Antibiotic, hypoglycemic, hypotensive, anthelmintic (eradicate worms from intestine), carminative (digestive), intestinal disinfectant (antiseptic), anti-rheumatic (pain killer and anti-inflammatory), corn remover, antimalarial, rubefacient (causing reddening of the skin), anti-oxidant, immune stimulant and lowers cholesterol.

Forms of use: Tincture, juice, poultice, raw.

Medicinal Uses

(a) (i) For cardiovascular disease and high blood pressure, use fresh garlic (10 cloves) or 500 mg garlic capsule twice daily.

(ii) Daily use of garlic alongwith salt and pepper keep one healthy and controls blood pressure.

(iii) A paste of garlic – one spoonful and honey – two spoonfuls if taken early in the morning on a roasted slice tones up the heart and maintains normal blood pressure.

(iv) Decreases incidence of thrombus formation.

(v) Activates the systemic circulation.

(b) Other Uses

Garlic is called poor man's remedy. It is useful in bronchial and asthmatic complaints. Garlic is antiseptic for intestinal ailments. In tubercular infection of the lungs, garlic juice diminishes the obstinate cough and acts as expectorant. It is also applied to indolent tumours. When given with common salt, garlic improves the nervous system and relieves headache, flatulence, hysteria etc. Garlic has also been found efficacious in sore throat, paralysis, gout, sciatica (pain in the course of the sciatic nerve) and many skin diseases. In the absence of common antibiotics, garlic juice may be applied to the open wounds to prevent bacterial infections and pus formation. The cloves have always been regarded as a source of strength. A decaying tooth will hurt less if packed with garlic pulp. It is aphrodisiac (capable of stimulating sexual impulse) and anti-cancerous in nature. A little rub behind the ear will alleviate the pain of trigeminal neuralgia, and a little pulp introduced into the ear will ease rheumatic otalgia (pain in the ear).

For all infections, add freshly chopped raw cloves to food three times daily or take garlic capsules.

3. Cassia absus, Linn.

Family : Caesalpiniaceae

Name : Hindi — Chaaksu

Sanskrit — Chaaksu

English	—	Chaaksu seeds
Bengali	—	Chaakut
Gujarati	—	Chimeru
Malayalam	—	Karinkolla
Tamil	—	Karun kanami
Trade name	—	Chaaksu bija

Description: Leaves compound, leaflets 1 to 2 inches long. Flowers reddish yellow, fruit 1 to 1½ inch long and slightly curved. Seed fine, compressed, lusturous and brownish black.

Distribution: An erect annual herb growing in lower parts of western Himalayas. Available in Indian Market.

Parts used: Seeds, Leaves.

Phytochemicals: Alkaloids, essential fatty acids, sterols and Chaaksu oil.

Properties: Bitter astringent, hypotensive and antibacterial.

Forms of use: Powder, juice, decoction.

Medicinal Uses

In blood pressure, Chaaksu is a wonderful remedy for bringing down high blood pressure. Powdered seeds 2-3 g soaked overnight- in a cup of water and filtered next day, if taken once or twice daily maintain blood pressure.

Other Uses

It is also considered to be a remedy for cough. Paste of seeds in bland oil cures ringworm and other skin diseases. Useful in purulent conjunctivitis, urinary bladder, treatment of wounds and sores. The drug is employed in certain diuretic drug formulations and a large number of eye lotions.

4. Rawolfia serpentine, (L) Bentham ex-kurz

Family	:	Apocyanaceae		
Name	:	Hindi	—	Chotachand
		Sanskrit	—	Sarpgandha

English	—	Serpentine
Bengali	—	Chander
Kannada	—	Sootvanti
Tamil	—	Chiran mal podi
Gujarati	—	Amal podi
Marathi	—	Aelakayi
Trade name	—	Sarpagandhaa

Description: An erect smooth shrub, 3.0-7.5 cm high, leaves whorled, 8-20 cm long, gradually tapering into short-petiole. Flowers about 1.5 cm long, petals white or pinkish, peduncle deep red, in small clusters. Fruits small, round dark purple or blackish when ripe.

Distribution: Found in all parts of India upto 1000 metre height. Available in Indian market.

Parts used: Root.

Properties: Bitter, tonic, sedative, febrifuge, heart stimulant, hypotensive, specific for insanity, Central Nervous System (CNS) depressant, stimulates the mammary gland etc.

Phytochemicals: Several alkaloids, sterols.

Forms of use: Powder, decoction

Medicinal Uses

(a) **Blood pressure/heart diseases**

The root of this plant contains several alkaloids which are proved affective in reducing the blood pressure. It is confirmed remedy for blood pressure associated with mild anxiety and pain in arms.

(b) **Other Uses**

It is sedative and hypnotic in nature and is used for insanity (Chronic mental illness), sexual aggression and intestinal disorder. The drug has tranquillising effect. The drug should not be given to persons suffering from bronchitis, asthma or gastric.

Decoction of the root is employed to increase uterine contraction and promote expulsion of the foetus.

In U.P. and Bihar, the plant root is sold as *Pagal-ki-dawa.* It's tiny root portion puts children to sleep in remote parts of Bihar (tribals).

5. Terminalia arjuna, Wight and Arn

Family	:	Combretaceae		
Name	:	Hindi	—	Arjun
		Sanskrit	—	Indradrum
		English	—	Arjuna myrobalan
		Bengali	—	Arjun
		Gujarati	—	Shadado
		Marathi	—	Ladada
		Kannada	—	Maddi
		Tamil	—	Vellai morudaa
		Trade name	—	Arjuna chaal

Description: Arjun is a large tree of 60-80 ft height. Leaves sub-opposite or alternate, sometimes clustered at the ends of the twigs and often bearing large glands on the petiole or near the base of the midrib beneath. Flowers small, green or white. Fruit ovoid, vary in size, smooth or angular or winged. Bark 5-10 mm thickness, external surface pink and inner surface reddish brown, finely striated.

Distribution: All over India.

Parts used: Stem Bark, Peeling out in thin flakes.

Properties: Astringent, lithotriptic, cardiac tonic, hypotensive.

Forms of use: Powder, decoction.

Medicinal Uses

(a) **In blood pressure/ heart diseases**

Arjuna is popularly used as cardiac tonic. The decoction of bark (3g), cane sugar (24g) with one cup cow's milk is a wonderful preparation for heart disease.

Powdered bark (2-3g) soaked overnight in a cup of water, decanted next morning and water taken empty stomach for bringing down the blood pressure.

(b) Other Uses

It is useful as diuretic, in cirrhosis (degeneration of liver), inflammatory conditions, dropsy and in the fracture of bones. The ash of bark is prescribed in scorpion sting. Fruit is a tonic and deobstruent. In doses of 14 to 28 ml in the form of decoction it is useful in haemorrhages, (bleeding), the escape of blood from any part of vascular system and other fluxes (an excessive fluid discharge from the body), also in diarrhoea, dysentery and sprue characterized by morning diarrhoea with bulky pale stool, anaemia, sore tongue, and failure to absorb fats.

Doses—	Decoction	—	60 to 120 ml
	Powder	—	1 to 3 g

Other Useful Plants

- *Dendrobium macraci* **(Jivanti)**—It is found to lower blood pressure in acute and chronic hypertension.
- *Digitalis purpurea* **(Tilpusphi)**—The main use of this drug is in heart diseases. The drug promotes and stimulates the activity of all muscular tissues. It is used in cases of congestive heart failure. It forces more blood into the coronaries and improves the nutrition of the heart. It helps in restoration and regulation of the function of the heart.
- *Crataegus oxyacantha*—Regulates heart rate and reduces high blood pressure. It is used in tincture and root extraction.
- *Camellia sinensis* **(Tea)**—Lowers blood pressure and cholesterol levels, strengthens capillaries.
- *Commiphora mukul* **(Guggul)**—Recommended for ischemic heart disease (defective flow of blood to the heart) and to bring down cholesterol level.
- *Solanium melongena* **(Baigan)**—Is an excellent cholesterol regulator.
- *Fumaria indica* **(Pitpapra)**—Is a definite remedy in low blood pressure.

- *Ephedra sinica*—Raises blood pressure.
- *Veratrum viride* **(Green Hellebore)**—Lowers blood pressure.
- *Solanum tuberosum* **(Potato)**—Helps regulate your heart beat, and research suggests that it can lower blood pressure and risk of stroke.

Persons suffering from low blood pressure i.e. if their blood pressure is lower than 120/70, one should take nutritive diets, vitamins, minerals, fruits, meat and soup etc.

Low blood pressure may be due to injury—internal or external leading to loss of blood, anaemia, acute or chronic diseases, food poisoning, leukaemia or other blood disorders.

Symptoms are extreme weakness, cold sweats, increased pulse and heart rate, giddiness and history of fainting, headache and chest pain.

Plants recommended in fall of blood pressure are: *Ephedra sinica, Eguisetum, Gerardiana* and *Fumaria indica.*

Blood pressure is a silent killer and to keep blood pressure in control and heart healthy, one has to follow certain norms. The first thing is that one has to change the lifestyle, food habits and exercises are to be made part of the life. This includes yoga, meditation, vegetarian diet and proper counselling.

Regular 20 minutes of aerobic exercises five days a week, this could be walking or cycling, say no to smoking and use of tobacco (as nicotine increases pulse rate), a vegetarian diet, tension free life controls blood pressure, sugar and cholesterol.

Medicines

Ayurvedic	:	Arjun tablet
Unani	:	Triyakfishar
Homeopathic	:	Glonine drops – 5-10 drops, 3 times daily.

4

Gastro-Intestinal Disorders

The stomach is one of the important organs of the body, necessary for the purpose of digestion and the assimilation of food which one consumes. As a result of the process the body will be nourished giving good health. The inner lining of the stomach is covered with mucus membrane consisting of small glands which secrete hydrochloric acid and enzymes. There are two ferments, namely renin and pepsin, present in the stomach juice which will help the food to break down into smaller particles or molecules. The hydrochloric acid also helps in the hydrolysis of the food that we take. The food which we consume is acted upon by bile, pancreatic juices, intestinal juices and finally bacteria, these juices make much smaller pieces for absorption. Water is absorbed in large intestine and residue passed through anus. This is the whole story of digestion.

Dyspepsia (Indigestion)

It includes various symptoms arising from the stomach, discomfort or pain, flatulence, nausea. There is sometimes a recognizable reason such as gastritis or gastric ulcer, but often indigestion is due to interferences with the normal working of the stomach by over-eating, eating when appetite has been suppressed by worry, anger, drugs, heavy smoking and unsuitable meals.

Diarrhoea

This is the condition when there is loose or watery stooling and one has to go to toilet a number of times. Most diarrhoea is due to inflammation of the intestine, with excessive production of watering mucus and over-activity of the intestinal muscles, both contributing to the symptoms. Inflammation can be caused by viruses (responsible for many outbreak of gastro-enteritis, especially in children), bacterial (bacterial food poisoning, bascillary dysentery), or larger parasites (amoebic dysentery, worm infestations), by irritant drugs and poisons, or by allergic reactions (food allergy, ulcerative colitis), due to malabsorption, sprue etc.

The functioning of the intestine is much influenced by the nervous system and endocrine glands (thyroid, adrenal), and disturbances of these may cause diarrhoea. Sustained fear or anxiety can lead to over-activity of the intestine. Irritable colon is a common complaint especially of people who worry about their bowels and take laxative.

Most of the common types of diarrhoea clear up in a day or two. If diarrhoea continues beyond this period and remains untreated it may cause severe dehydration (especially if vomiting is there). So till medical aid is not reached sugar-salt water solution (sugar+a pinch of salt/cold drink/sharbat should be given to the sick).

Dysentery

It is a condition wherein the patient notices mucus and blood in the stool together with abdominal pain and tenesmus (a painful endeavour to defecate or urinate). In other words, dysentery is a collection of symptoms indicating severe irritation of the large intestine. It is of two kinds:

(a) amoebic dysentery (it is due to the infection of large intestine with *Entamoeba histolytica,* a protozoa and where patient passes stool with mucus).

(b) bascillary dysentery (caused by bacterial *shigella* where patient passes stool with blood).

Amoebic dysentery if goes untreated it may cause liver abscess and amoebic hepatitis.

Constipation

Constipation is the most over-rated of all symptoms. Because faeces are unpleasant and seemingly poisonous, people have always believed that getting rid of them as fast as possible must promote health. Infact, getting rid of poisons is mainly the job of kidneys. Faeces are poisonous in the sense that they contain bacteria that can cause trouble if they contaminate parts of the body other than intestine. But in the intestine these bacteria are harmless, and in any case they can not be eliminated by purges.

Though most people open their bowels once a day there is no need for everyone to do so. In countries with a poor but bulky diet, the natural average may be two or three motions a day, but plenty of people stay healthy on two or three motions a week. With the richer, less bulky diets of wealthy societies some people open their bowels much less often without being in any real sense constipated.

On the other hand, a daily motion is no proof that one is not constipated, because the rectum may not be completely empty itself.

Normal bowel function has two components. Waste-matter in the whole of the large intestine finds its way to the rectum without undue delay, and the rectum is completely emptied at more or less regular intervals. Failure of either is constipation.

The effects of constipation are mechanical. Discomfort, disinclination to exert or interest oneself and the rest are reflex symptoms of distension of the rectum. They could equally well be caused by air in the rectum, and have nothing to do with poisoning. If faeces stagnate and harden, their passage may injure the anus and cause cracked skin (fissure), blood blister (external piles), or distended veins (internal piles). Motions then become painful, and the constipation becomes worse. It is in these cases more than any others that purgatives are needed. Much constipation is due either to faulty diet—the "easily digested" foods of western style are all too easily digested and leave no residue—or to mental and physical sluggishness. The easiest remedies are vegetables and exercise. The psychological factor is important but hard to define, worry about constipation may be the main element. The regular use of purgatives irritate the intestine, which in time becomes accustomed to its delay dose and will not perform without drugs, thus imiginary constipation becomes real.

Though constipation is not an important illness in itself, it may be a symptom of something more serious. Constipation does not cause cancer, but cancer of the large intestine causes the bowels to be opened less (or more) often than has been usual for the particular patient. Prompt investigation of this symptom is often life saving, for these cancers are generally curable in the early stages when symptoms are first noticed.

Symptoms

Symptoms requiring medical attention and treatment (Stomach and intestines)—

- Recent loss of appetite or aversion to particular food.
- Difficulty in swallowing.
- Severe vomiting, especially if includes blood.
- Sudden pain in the upper abdomen temporary relieved by biscuits, food or milk.
- Sudden pain in the upper abdomen in the middle of the night.
- Weakness or dizziness before or after passing a jet black stool.
- Recent change in bowel habbits—alternating constipation and diarrhoea.
- Irregular bleeding before, during or after passing stool.
- Severe pain around the navel, which shifts to the right-side of the abdomen.

Treatment

Many plant preparations are available in the market to

correct all types of gastro-intestinal problems.

Role of Plants

1. Cephaelis ipecacuanha (Brot) A. Rich

Family	:	Rubiaceae	
Names	:	Hindi	— Ipecac
		English	— Ipecac

Description: A small trailing herb. Root slender, spreading horizontally. Mature roots monitiform, in bunches. Leaves in opposite pairs, their tips pointed, margins entire. Flowers white, small in small bunches.

Distribution: Cultivated in India. Available in the market.

Parts used: Rhizome.

Properties: Appetizer, anti-amoebic, anti-cough, emetic (causing vomiting), diaphoretic (producing sweat).

Phytochemicals: Alkaloid-emetine (Main active substance).

Forms of use: Tincture, powder, decoction, syrup.

Medicinal Uses

The rhizome of the plant constitute the drug Ipecae. This drug is useful in amoebic dysentery and diarrhoea with abdominal pain and tenesmus.

Given in large doses, it brings about vomiting and this property is utilized for bringing relief from cough. It also acts as a diaphoretic i.e., brings about sweating.

Syrup ipecae was one of the drugs to act as an emetic to expel orally ingested poisons.

2. Holarrhena antidysenterica (Roth) DC.

Family	:	Apocyanace	
Names	:	Hindi	— Kurchi
		Sanskrit	— Kalinga

English	— Conessi seed
Bengali	— Titaa indrajau
Marathi	— Kadoo indrajau
Gujarati	— Kadvo indrajau
Tamil	— Kulappaalaivisai
Trade name	— Indrajau karwaa

Description: A small shrub or small tree, sometimes upto 10 m tall. Leaves 10-30 cm long, ovate, thin, nerves on the leaves conspicuous. Leaf stalks very small. Flowers white, fragrant, 1-15 cm diameter, in large terminal bunches. Fruits slender, cylindric, 20-45 cm long, 6-8 mm thick, dark grey with white speeks all over. Seeds about 1 cm long, having a tuft of long (2-25 cm), brown hairs at top. All parts of the plant, on an incision give out white milky juice.

Distribution: The plant occurs throughout India. Available in Indian market as "Kurchi".

Parts used: Bark, seeds and leaves.

Properties: Bitter, stomachic, astringent, powerful anti-dysentric, febrifuge, anthelmintic and carminative.

Forms of use: Decoction, powder.

Phytochemicals: Terpenes, alkaloids, sterols, saponins, tanins and flavones.

Medicinal Uses

1. The dried bark of the plant constitutes the drug "kurchi". The chief use of this drug is in amoebic dysentery. Liquid extract of the bark has a good effect in dysentery and intermittent fevers.
2. The bark of the plant also has tonic and febrifuge properties.
3. The alkaloid contents present in the bark has been found to retard growth of tubercular bacilli.
4. Bark of the stem and root, preferably of the young plants and the seeds, is used as a remedy in acute and chronic diarrhoea and dysentery. Seeds enter into the composition

of many prescription for bilious affections, fever, bowel complaints, piles and intestinal worms.

3. Euphorbia hirta, Linn.

Family	:	Euphorbiaceae	
Names	:	Hindi	— Lal dudhi
		Sanskrit	— Dugudhika
		Bengali	— Barokheruie
		Marathi	— Dudhi, mothi dudhi
		Gujarati	— Dudeli
		Telugu	— Bidarie
		Tamil	— Amam patchaiarisi
		Malayalam	— Nela palai

Description: A small perennial herb with milky latex in all parts of the plant. Stems hairy, leaves small, opposite, elliptic-oblong or oblong lanceolate, fruits small, seeds smooth and blue coloured.

Distribution: Throughout hotter parts of India.

Parts used: Whole plant.

Properties: Anthelmintic, expectorant, antidysentric, hypoglycemic.

Phytochemicals: Alkaloid, essential oil, phenols, sterol, flavones and fatty acids.

Forms of use: Decoction, infusion, paste and juice.

Medicinal Uses

1. Juice of the plant is useful in dysentery. At least 5-10 plants are to be collected and made into a paste with some water. It is filtered and taken two or three times a day. It is a confirmed treatment for dysentery, abdominal pain and tenesmus.
2. The plant as a whole is used in diseases of children in worms, bowel complaints, cough etc.
3. Decoction of the plant is given in broncheal affections and asthma.

4. Latex of the plant is used as application for warts.

Doses—

Infusion ... 14 to 28 ml
Decoction ... 28 to 56 ml

4. Aegle marmelos Linn. Correa

Family : Rutaceae

Names : Hindi — Bael
Sanskrit — Bilva
English — Bael fruit
Bengali — Bel mool chaal
Gujarati — Bilinu jor chaal
Kannada — Bil patte
Malayalam — Koovlam mulam toli
Trade name — Bilva mool chaal

Description: A medium sized tree bearing strong auxillary thorn. Leaves with 3 or 5 leaflets. Flowers greenish white, sweet scented, about 2.5 cm across, in small bunches. Fruit 8-20 cm diameter, globose, green, finally greyist, round woody, pulp orange-coloured, sweet, aromatic.

Distribution: Found all over India. Readily available in the market during summer.

Parts used: Fruit (ripe and unripe both), root bark, stem, leaves, rind of the ripe fruit and flowers.

Properties: Sweet, aromatic, cooling, alterant, nutritive and laxative. Unripe fruit astringent, digestive and stomachic.

Phytochemicals: Glycosides, alkaloids, flavone.

Forms of use: Jam, sharbat, decoction, powder.

Medicinal Uses

1. It is useful in chronic dysentery and diarrhoea, particularly for patients having diarrhoea with spells of constipation. For this a ripe fruit is eaten.
2. Sweet drinks (Sharbats) prepared from the ripe fruits are

useful as soothing agent for intestine of patients who have just recovered from bascillary dysentery.

3. The unripe or half ripe fruits improve appetite and digestion.
4. The bael fruit is valuable chiefly for its mucilage and pectin, it removes constipation if fruit is taken continuously for a few days.
5. A decoction of the leaves is a febrifuge and expectorant (antibiotic activity of the leaf, fruit and root is confirmed experimentally) especially in asthmatic complaints.
6. Decoction of the root bark is used in intermittent fevers, melancholia (a mental illness in which the predominant symptom is depression, unhappiness and misery), palpitation of heart and inflammation of uterus
7. Ripe fruit removes constipation and dysentery. Powdered pulp is given in doses of 2 to 4 g in acute dysentery with gripping pain.

Doses—

Powder ... 2 to 4 g
Infusion ... 2 to 12 ml
Decoction ... 28 to 56 ml

Other Useful Plants

- ***Zingiber afficinale* (Adrak)**—Extremely valuable in dyspepsia, colic, flatulence (presence of excessive of gas in stomach and alimentary canal), vomiting, spasm and other painful affections of the stomach. It should be used in food stuff.
- ***Terminalia chebula* (Harr), *Terminalia bellerica* (Bahera) and *Emblica officinalis* (Amla)**—Together called TRIPHALA (3 Fruits)- an Ayurvedic remedy for treating various gastro-intestinal disorders. Two teaspoonfuls triphala powder each night clears constipation and allied complaints.

- *Allium salivum* **(Lahsun)**—An ancient intestinal antiseptic expels gas from the stomach and cleans the alimentary canal. A paste of 5 cloves mixed with honey taken daily on a bread improves appetite, digestion and removes flatulence.
- *Mentha arvensis* **(Podina)**—Is useful in indigestion, tenesmus, diarrhoea and vomiting. It is being used in the form of liquid and chutney.
- *Nigella sativa* **(Kanlaunji)**—This is useful in stomach trouble—50 gms of kanlaunji is soaked in vineger, dried and powdered. This powder 6-10 gm when used after meals clears gas and indigestion and gives strength to stomach, spleen, kidney.
- *Amorphophallus companulatus* **(Zamikand)**—It is used in piles and given as a restorative in dyspepsia and debility. It is a hot carminative in the form of a pickle.
- *Foeniculum vulgare* **(Soya)**—It is useful in indigestion, colic, flatulence. It should be eaten during the cultivated season.
- *Cuminum cyminum* **(Zeera)**—In indigestion, loss of appetite, flatulence, bloated feeling—50 gms zeera (black or white) soaked in vineger and dried. To it add 6 gm powdered dried ginger and 4 gm black salt. Use this mixture 20-25 gms after meals.
- *Plantago ovata* **(Isafgol)**—Is useful in dysentery and chronic diarrhoea. It is also useful as a soothing agent for mucous membranes and removes constipation.

Medicines

Ayurvedic

Diarrhoea and Dysentery	— Katujarist (for blood dysentery), Amibica
Indigestion	— Lavan Bhaskar Churna and Hingavasti Churna
Constipation	— Triphala, Kabzhar

Unani

Indigestion	— Pachnol and Majoon Mukavy Meda
Diarrhoea and Dysentery	— Pech, Malti basant, Jawarish Amla
Constipation	— Kurs Mulayyan, Majoon-Anjir and Isafgol

Homeopathic

Diarrhoea	— China Complex
Indigestion	— Hydrastis Complex
Dysentery	— Merce Sol Complex

5

Intestinal Worms and Related Diseases

The worms to be considered here are those that live in the human intestine. The common intestinal worms of childhood are passed from person to person; faeces contain the eggs; a child's become contaminated; he swallows the eggs and the cycle is repeated. The worms of this type include the round worms–Ascaris, the thread worms–Enterobius. The eggs of the thread worms are laid on the skin around the anus, where they cause itching. The child scratches and reinfects himself when he sucks his fingers. Otherwise these worms cause little trouble, except that rare case of blockage by a tangle of worms in the intestine are described.

Another type of worms are hook and tapeworms. Hookworms can occur in most parts of the world, but because of the mode of infection they are common only in tropical countries. The larvae live in soil contaminated by faeces, and enter the body through the skin of the feet. Therefore the infection thrives only where sanitation and personal hygiene are defective and people walk bare-footed.

The tapeworms are like long segmented ribbons and are a parasite of cattle, pig and fish. With adequate meat inspection these parasites do not often reach the consumer, and with thorough cooking even infected food is rendered harmless.

Symptoms

- Black ring around eyes
- Inflated belly
- Nausea

- Drooping of saliva during sleep
- Grinding of teeth in night
- Convulsions
- Anaemia
- Increased appetite but no weight gain
- Itching around nose
- Urticaria (nettle rash)
- Itching around anus

Causes

- Use of unwashed vegetables
- Unhygenic conditions
- Bare foot walking
- Use of excess sweets
- Soil eating

A number of plants are found useful in expelling worms from the intestine. Such few plants are described here.

Role of Plants

1. Artemisia maritima. Linn.

Family	:	Asteraceae	
Names	:	Hindi	— Kirmala
		Sanskrit	— Gadadhari
		English	— Absinthin
		Marathi	— Kirmaniova
		Kashmiri	— Maxrni
		Trade name—	Wormseed; Santonica

Description: A stout, much branched, perennial aromatic shrub, about 3 ft. high. Leaves 2-5 cm. long, whitish in colour, divided into numerous fine, linear segments, upper leaves simple, undivided linear. Flower heads small, in short spikes.

Distribution: The plant occurs in northern India from Kashmir to kumaon.

Parts used: Flowers, buds and leaves.

Properties: Antiperiodic, aperient (describing drugs which have a laxative action), stomachic, tonic, anthelmintic and cardiac stimulant.

Phytochemicals: Terpenes, lactone-Santonin.

Forms of use: Powder, decoction.

Medicinal Uses

(a) It is powerful anthelintic and this property is due to the presence of a chemical santonin. Powdered young leaves when taken expel thread and round worms from the intestine.

(b) Other uses

The drug is useful in fevers, dropsy and as a stimulant, a fomentation of the herb is applied over inflammations, tumours and foul ulcers.

2. Centratherum anthelminticum, Wild, Kuntze

Family	:	Asteraceae	
Names	:	Hindi	— Banjira, Somraj
		Sanskrit	— Somaraji
		Bengali	— Somraj
		Gujarati	— Kalijiri
		Telugu	— Adavijilakara
		Malayalam	— Kattu-jirakam
		Marathi	— Kalenjiri
		Tamil	— Kattu-shiragarm
		Kannada	— Kadu-jirage

Description: An erect tall herb, stems and leaves covered with minute hairs. Leaves 6-10 cm long, their margins toothed, base tapering into a petiole. Flower heads 1.5-2.5 cm diameter, in small clusters, each head with 30-40 minute purplish flowers. Fruits, which are scientifically called achenes, 4.5-6 mm long, cylindric, hairy with 10 narrow ridges, the tuft of hairs on top of achenes, reddish.

Distribution: The plant is found throughout India upto an altitude of about 1,500 m, and is more common in waste places near habitations and around where dirty water flows.

Parts used: All parts of the plant and seeds.

Properties: Anthelmintic, tonic, stomachic and diuretic.

Phytochemicals: Bitter substance, sterols, fatty acids and essential oils.

Forms of use: Powder, leaf juice, decoction.

Medicinal Uses

(a) The word anthelminticum in the name of this plant suggests the medicinal usage of this plant in treatment of worms. It is useful in worm infections. Powdered seeds 0.5 g to 1 g given to ward off thread worms even if their administration is not followed by a purgative. It's utility in thread worms infections has been confirmed by trials in hospital.

(b) Other Uses

In old literature, the plant has been reported to be useful also as stimulant and antiseptic and for promoting urination. It is found to be useful in skin diseases and in scorpion stings.

3. Chenopodium ambrosioides, Linn

Family	:	Chenopodiaceae	
Names	:	Hindi	— Bathu ka sag
		Sanskrit	— Sugandhavastak
		English	— Indian wormseed
		Kannada	— Kaaduvoma
		Malayalam	— Kattayamodagum
		Tamil	— Katta sambadam
		Telugu	— Pappukura

Description: An erect, much branched herb, 1 to 2 ft high with aromatic grandular hairs, leaves short, petioled, oblong, or lancealate, flowers small green, in axiallary and terminal panicled leafy spikes, fruits are somewhat smooth, slightly compressed, with a thin pericap surrounding the seeds. Seeds are small, brown, smooth and shining and possess a bitter pungent taste.

Distribution: Found all over India in wheat field during winter season.

Parts Used: Whole plant.

Properties: Anthelmintic, laxative, amoebicide (an agent capable of destroying amoebae).

Phytochemicals: The oil contains ascaridole content. A terpene-chenopodium oil.

Forms of use: Decoction, leaves mixed with pulses forming a tasteful curry of Dal + Sag. Boiled whole plant is also eaten with salt. Bread is prepared by mixing leaves with flour.

Medicinal Uses

(a) It is a powerful anthelmintic expelling almost all types of intestinal worms.

(b) Preparation of Dal-Sag when used for 3/4 days. It will expel all types of obstinate worms from the intestine. No laxative is needed. It works better than allopathic preparations.

(c) Boiled Bathu Ka Sag when eaten with salt also quickly removes *enterobius* (thread worm) and *ascaris* (kechua) from the intestine.

Other Uses

It has also been found useful in the treatment of amoebic dysentery. It is a perfect laxative. So, if dried in powder form, it can be used mixing with Isafgol.

Doses—

Oil — 3 to 12 ml.

Other Useful Plants

- ***Carica papaya* (Papita)**—The seeds are found to be strong anthelmintic, they are given with honey for expelling round worms. The leaves are also anthelmintic.

- *Ambelia tsjeriam*—**Cottom (Baibirang)**—The dried fruit of the plant constituted the drug, effective against tapeworms and roundworms. The drug also showed some antibacterial and antitubercular activity.
- *Euphorbia hirta* **(Dudhi)**—It is useful in removing worms in children. The plant is also found to be antibacterial and anti-tubercular experimentally.
- *Gaultheria fragrantissima* **(Gandhpura Ka Tel, Oil of winter green)**—It is useful against hookworms. The oil of the plant is used in many preparations for killing or repelling mosquitoes, flies and other insects.
- *Mallotus phillippaensis* **(Kamela)**—Kamela is chiefly used for destroying tapeworms. The kamela powder is taken with milk or curd etc. If one dose of kamela does not expel the worms, the dose is repeated. Sometimes a dose of castor oil is necessary to expel the dead worms. It is also useful in skin diseases and hairs of fruit reduce fertility.
- *Curcuma longa* **(Haldi)**—One gram haldi powder if used with warm water, two times a day kills pinworms and roundworms.
- *Ananas comosus* **(Ananas)**—Fresh juice of the leaves or leaves are powerfully purgative, anthelmintic and vermicide. Mixture of chuhara+Ajwain+Baibarang (1:1:1), if taken (6 g) with honey two/three times a day clears worms in children.

The worms attach themselves to the wall of intestine and cause very slight but persistent loss of blood. The resulting anaemia is not severe but it is enough to keep the patient's general condition below what it should be. But above all general hygiene is essential and bare foot walking should be discouraged.

Medicines

Ayurvedic	:	Krimghna Vati/Vidangarista
Unani	:	Kirmar
Homeopathic	:	Santonine Complex

6

Urinary Diseases

Urinary diseases include mainly diseases of the kidneys, ureter, urinary bladder and urethra. In the urinary system, there are a pair of large excretory glands (two bean shaped kidneys) at the back of the abdomen (in the lumber region) concerned primarily with regulating the amount of water in the body. All life is aquatic. The simplest animal, the amoeba, lives under water. It's cell membrane is a leaky structure: it prevents the body substance or protoplasm from escaping, but water can diffuse in and out of the amoeba, as can salts and other simple chemical substances dissolved in the water.

The amoeba takes up substances from its environment to be incorporated into its own body substance, and the chemical processes of life create unwanted byproducts which would poison the cell if allowed to accumulate. Foods and waste products are exchanged by simple diffusion, which depends on the tendency of molecules in a fluid to move from zones of high concentration to zones of low concentration. Provided that the water in which the amoeba lives contains the right substances in the right proportions, both supply and waste-disposal are passive and automatic.

The only problem is the water itself. Sea-water is rather too strong a solution of salts etc., and fresh water is much too dilute for the need of living animals. Simple diffusion has to be supplemented by active selection, animals living in sea-water retain more water than simple diffusion would allow, and animals in fresh water reject it, so that the solution inside the cell is kept at the right strength. In either case this solution is equivalent to somewhat diluted sea-water.

Although a man does not live in water, each of the millions of cells of which he is built must do. More than half of his body weight is water, most of it is inside the cells, a little in the blood, and some 12 litres is tissue fluid, which permeates every minute crevice and bathes every cell.

No living cell can withstand much change in its environment. Even slight changes in acidity or concentration will kill a highly developed structure such as a human nerve cell. The organs mainly responsible for preventing such changes are the kidneys.

Man has two kidneys, one at each side of the back bone between the thick muscles of the back and the abdomen. It is the size of a cupped hand, about 4½ inches from top to bottom and 2½ inches from side to side, it is 1 to 1½ inches thick.

Functions of the Kidneys: Filteration of the blood to remove toxins and impurities from the blood are the functions of the kidneys. And apart from it, kidneys also control-regulate blood pressure and they produce a hormone—erythropoietin, which controls the rate at which red blood cells are formed in the bone marrow. The urine will be excreted from the kidneys through the uretor which opens into the bladder and through the urethra outside. Substances such as sodium, potassium, calcium, magnessium, amino acids and chlorine are reabsorbed into the system and are thrown out through the urine in the form of phosphates, urea and uric acids. When the kidney fails to excrete all these things, then toxic materials like uric acid will accumulate in the blood and urea resulting in "Uraemia". The kidney regulates the water and electrolytic content of the body, and maintains the normal acid-base equilibrium of the blood and retention of the other substances vital to the body e.g. glucose, amino acids, phosphates, bicarbonates and proteins. Glucose is normally reabsorbed by the system completely by the proximat tubules. The kidney excesses the waste products of metabolism and toxic substances. The end products of metabolism are proteins, urea, uric acid, creatine, phosphates-sulphates.

It also regulates the blood pressure and they produce a hormone which controls the rate at which red blood cells are formed in the bone marrow.

In health and in average condition a man passes about 1.5 litres of urine daily, but this amount may vary which should not be less than 600 ml to carry out waste products. Fear, depression and shivering can increase the out-put of urine but soon things return to normalcy except if one is not suffering from diabetes insipidus (discussed in chapter 1).

Disorders: One normal kidney is enough to maintain good health, two kidneys can tolerate a good deal of damage. Even with advanced kidney disease the symptoms are often mild and vague until a very late stage. If the kidneys stop working altogether the patient quickly succumbs to acidosis and poisoning by waste products unless he can be treated.

Kidney disorders may be due to hypertension, pyelitis (infection), oedema (dropsy), congenital defects, injuries, tuberculosis, bright's diseases (nephritis), stone formation and tumours.

Symptoms

- Blood in urine.
- Obstruction in passing urine.
- Scanty and painful urination.
- White urination deposited on the ground.
- Protein in urine.
- Accumulation of water in the body.
- Puffiness under eyes.
- Albumin in urine.
- Anaemia, loss of appetite.
- Severe pain in back.
- Nagging pain in the loins and if urine has smoky appearance.
- Difficulty in starting the stream or inability to project it as before.

Renal Colic

Small stones or gravel may pass easily down the ureters and be voided in the urine or remain in the bladder. Larger stones may become impacted in the ureter or only pass with great difficulty giving rise to renal colic. Before this condition arises, the patient complains of an aching loin, with occasional attacks of more colicy pain. Urine has to be passed frequently and is usually blood stained. When the stone begins to pass down the ureter, the pain increases to agony, cold sweat, temperature, rapid pulse until stone suddenly passes and pain ceases.

Treatment

Apart from various approaches to kidney treatment and surgery, plants also offer to great extent, a herbal way to alleviate these conditions.

Role of Plants

1. Tribulus terrestris Linn.

Family	:	Zygophyllaceae		
Names	:	Hindi	—	Chota-gokhru
		Sanskrit	—	Laghu Gokshura
		English	—	Small caltrops
		Bengali	—	Gokhuri mool
		Gujarati	—	Betha gokhara mool
		Marathi	—	Sategokhru mool
		Tamil	—	Nerunje vera
		Kannada	—	Neggillumullu
		Trade name	—	Gokharumool

Description: A prostrate spreading herb, densely covered with minute hair. Leaves in opposite pairs, 5-8 cm long, compound, leaflets 4-7 pairs, 8-12 mm long. Flowers pale yellow, 1-15 cm diameter, growing solitary opposite to the leaves or in axils of leaves. Fruit very characteristic and easily known by numerous spines on it. Fruits often cling to clothes, bodies of animals and wheels of vehicles. Seeds many in each of the five parts of the fruit.

Distribution: The plants occur throughout India.

Parts used: Fruit, root and whole plant.

Properties: Cooling, demulcent (a substance which protects the mucous membranes and allays irritations), diuretic, tonic and aphrodisiac.

Phytochemicals: Alkaloid, aromatic substance, unsaturated acids, essential oil, large amount of nitrates (mainly responsible for diuretic action), harmon and harmin.

Forms of use: Decoction, powder, infusion.

Medicinal Uses

1. Plant and dried spiny fruits are used in decoction or infusion in all the diseases of genito-urinary system such as difficulty in passing urine (dysuria), inflammation of the bladder, caused by infection (chronic cystitis), formation of small stones in kidney (calculous and grovel affections), urinary disorders, kidney diseases and suppression of urine.
2. The action of the drug on the mucous membrane of the urinary track has confirmed diuretic properties (as per clinical tests).
3. Decoction of the fruits with addition of carbonate of potash is given in painful micturition passing of urine.

Other Uses

1. Fruits are used in sexual weakness.
2. An infusion of the fruits is useful in gout.
3. It is also used in cough, diseases of the heart.

2. Raphnus sativus, Linn

Family	:	Crufiferae		
Names	:	Hindi	—	Muli
		Sanskrit	—	Moolaka

English	—	Radish
Bengali	—	Muli
Marathi	—	Mula
Gujarati	—	Mura
Tamil	—	Mullangi
Telugu	—	Mullangi
Kannada	—	Mullangi
Malayalam	—	Mullangi

Description: An annually cultivated plant, leaves very deeply lobed, end broad. Taproot long, thick white. Flowers white or lilac with purple veins.

Distribution: Cultivated throughout India.

Parts used: Seeds, root and leaves.

Properties: Diuretic, laxative, lithotriptic and antiscorbutic (a remedy for scurvy or minor degree of vit. C deficiency).

Phytochemicals: Flavonoids, essential oil, glucoside, enzyme, methyl mercaptan, carbohydrates and mineral etc.

Forms of use: Juice, root powder, decoction.

Medicinal Uses

1. Leaf juice is prescribed in difficulty of passing urine (dysuria), closure of urinary passage (stranguary), (calculi).
2. Root juice prescribed in urinary trouble.
3. Seeds are found to be effective in increasing information and excretion.

Other Uses

1. Leaf juice acts as stimulant.
2. Seeds are useful as carminative, expectorant, laxative.
3. Root juice also prescribed for piles and stomachache.

3. Solanum surattens. Burm, f.

Family	:	Solanaceae		
Names	:	Hindi	—	Bhatkatayia mool

Sanskrit	—	Kantakari
English	—	Kantakari
Bengali	—	Kantkaari mool
Telugu	—	Challanmulaga veru
Gujarati	—	Bhoyaringaninu jar
Tamil	—	Kandangattari vera
Trade name	—	Kateli ki jar

Description: A prickly, much branched herb, usually spreading or diffused, young branches densely covered with minute star shaped hairs, prickles yellow, shining, about 1.5 cm long. Leaves upto 10 cm long, their midribs and other nerves with sharp yellow prickles. Flowers purple, about 2 cm long, few together in small bunches opposite the leaves. Fruit 1.5-2 cm, round yellow or pale with green veins.

Distribution: Throughout India on waste places, on roadside.

Parts Used: Whole plant.

Properties: Diuretic, carminative (a drug which is used to facilitate the eructation of gas from stomach), expectorant, febrifuge, bitter, digestive, alterant and astringent.

Phytochemicals: Alkaloids.

Forms of Use: Decoction, powder.

Medicinal Uses

It is diuretic and is considered useful in concretions or stones in bladders.

Other Uses

1. A decoction of the plant is used in gonorrhoea and rheumatism.
2. A fine powder of the fruits with honey is useful for chronic cough in children.
3. The drug is used in cough, asthma, pain in chest, fever and sore throat.

Other Useful Plants

- *Psoralea corylifolia* **(Babchi)**—The seeds are useful for promoting urination.
- *Luffa acutangula* **(Turai)**—It is effective diuretic. It stimulates the mucous membrane of the kidneys and urinary passage.
- *Taraxacum officinale* **(Dudal)**—Root is useful in chronic disorder of the kidney.
- *Hyoscyamus niger* **(Ajwain)**—Useful in urinary affections as irritation of the kidneys.
- *Asparagus racemosus* **(Satavari)**—Also prescribed in kidney ailments.
- *Ocimum sanctum* **(Tulsi)**—Seeds are useful in complaints of urinary system.
- *Hygrophila auriculata* **(Talmakhana)**—It is useful in the disease of urino-genital system. The diuretic activity of the drug is believed to be due to combination of both inorganic and organic contents of the plants. Seeds and roots, singly also, have diuretic property.
- *Boehavia diffusa* **(Bishkopra)**—The main use of the drug is as a diuretic i.e., to promote urination in dropsy and urinary problems.
- *Nigella sativa* **(Kalaunji)**—It is useful in kidney and bladder stones.

Keeping kidneys healthy does not involve too much effort. All you need to do is

- Control diabetes (if it is there) and high B.P.
- Don't take drugs unnecessarily.
- Watch your urinary symptoms.
- Pain in the back just below the ribs.

Prevention

- 8 glasses of water/soups/juices/milk.

- Eating calcium.
- Avoid meat in excess.
- Take plenty of potassium, magnessium and vitamin B_6 present in bananas, potatoes, corn and Soyabeans.
- Stop smoking.
- Cutting salt in your diet.
- Exercise to speed up blood circülation.

Medicines

Ayurvedic	:	Cystone
Unani	:	Kushta Hajrul Yahood
Homeopathic	:	Berberis-Vulgaris-30 Canthris-30 alternate with 2 hrs difference.

7

Management of Cancer: Herbal Approaches

Cancer should be called a symptom rather than disease. It indicates the abnormal uncontrolled and rapid growth of cells. Because of this, cancer cells are malignant in nature. Cancer cells differ from normal biological cells mainly in two ways. Firstly, so long as the host is alive, cancer cells are also alive and rapidly multiply themselves to form new cancer cells. They do not die until host dies. But in case of ordinary cells, they after a cycle decay automatically. Secondly, cancer cells can undergo "Metastasis". The term metastasis means transfer of cancer cells from one organ of the body to another not directly connected with it. All malignant cells are capable of metastasizing, which means forming new loci in a distant part of the body from the original position. Ordinary cells on the other hand have no such power of metastasis. No stomach cell can move to the heart or heart cells to brain and so on.

There are more than 100 types of cancer. But broadly speaking, they are of two types: (1) Caricinoma, meaning malignant new growth made up of epithelial cells tending to infilterate surrounding tissues and give rise to metastasis and (b) SARCOMA means cancer arising in bone, connective tissue or muscle, i.e., the tissues mainly derived in the embryo from mesoderm and lymphatic blood vessels.

There are three methods for treating cancer: (1) Surgery, which can not be used when there is metastasis, (2) radiation therapy, which affects normal and cancerous tissues equally and (3) chemotherapy with some side effects. There is of course, another way of treatment, the immunotherapy—

the manipulation of immune response which is still in its infancy. Immunotherapy is often tried in association with chemotherapy.

In chemotherapy, the main basic factor in inhibition and cure of cancer lies in the ability of drugs or chemotherapeutic agents to kill cancer cell. These drugs have, however, no capacity of repairing or converting a cancer cell to a normal one. Our major difficulty here is that we yet do not know the exact cause of growth of cancer cells.

Symptoms

- Any sore that does not heal.
- A lump or thickening in the breast or elsewhere.
- Unusual bleeding or discharge.
- Any change in a wart or mole.
- Persistant indigestion or difficulty in swallowing
- Persistant hoarseness or cough.
- Any change in normal bowel habits.

Cause

Apparent cause is chewing of tobacco and tobacco products, pollution and exposure to radiations otherwise in most of the cases cause is unknown.

The role of cancer medicines is undoubtedly remarkable owing to the increasing scope and complexity of cytotoxic drugs. In this connection, a large number of plants have been tried and quite a good number of them have been used with success.

Role of Plants

1. Viola odorata, Linn

Family	:	Violaceae		
Names	:	Hindi	—	Banafshah
		Sanskrit	—	Banafsha
		English	—	Wild violet
		Bengali	—	Banafshah
		Marathi	—	Bag a banasa

Gujarati	—	Banaphsa
Tamil	—	Vialettu
Kannada	—	Violethoo
Trade name	—	Sweet-Violet

Description: This herbaceous perennial plant has a short rhizome and creeping stolons which put out roots. The petiolate basal leaves are in rosette form mid-green in colour. They are kidney-shaped with a corrugate surface, well defined venation and a crenate margin. The flowers are reddish brown. The fruit is a sub-spherical capsule containing dark seeds which have an outgrowth at one side.

Distribution: A herb found in kashmir and in the temperate western Himalyas above 5000 ft. It is readily available in the market.

Parts used: Leaves, stem and flowers.

Phytochemicals: Flowers and root contain an alkaloid-violine, a glycoside-violuquercetin. Roots, leaves and blossoms contain methyl salicylate in the form of glucoside. Flowers also contain volatile oil. Roots and rhizomes contain an alkaloid-odoratine.

Properties: Emetic, purgative, emollient (any substance that softens the skin and renders it more pliant), demulcent (a substance which protects the mucous membranes and allays irritation), diaphoretic, diuretic, antipyretic, febrifuge, expectorant, laxative and anti-cancerous.

Form of Use: Flower infusion, decoction and juice-syrup.

Medicinal Uses

(a) In cancer: The fresh leaves of *Viola odorate* is a reputed drug for treatment of cancer. Leaves relieve pain of cancerous growth, especially of throat, 2.5 oz of the fresh leaves are infused in a pint of boiling water in a covered metallic jar for 12 hours; the strained liquid is taken in the course of a day, in doses of a full glass at a time for the treatment of cancer of throat and tongue.

(b) Other Uses

1. The leaves are emollient and laxative. Powdered leaves taken at bed time with plain water, for constipation.
2. The underground root is emetic and purgative; an infusion made with 2 oz of the roots act as a purge and emetic; its juice causes nausea and vomiting.
3. The flowers are given in bilious affection, epilepsy, nervous disorders, prolapse of the rectum and uterus, and inflammatory swelling. The flowers are popularly used as a diaphoretic and for the treatment of coughs, sore throat, kidney diseases and liver disorders. It is used either as an infusion or as syrup.

Doses—

Flower infusion	- 30 to 50ml.
Decoction of leaves	- 500ml to 1 litre

2. Catharanthus roseus (L) G. Don

Family	:	Apocynaceae		
Names	:	Hindi	–	Sadabahar
		Bengali	–	Nayantara
		Oriya	–	Ainskati
		Malayalam	–	Ushamalari
		Marathi	–	Sada-phul
		Telugu	–	Billagannesu
		Tamil	–	Sudukadu mallikal

Description: An erect herb upto one metre high, leaves orate, opposite, flowers in axillary clusters of 2 or 3 petals white or purple-red type. Fruits-many seeded, follicles.

Distribution: The plant is found all over India and cultivated in garden.

Parts used: Root and leaves.

Phytochemicals: Alkaloids-vincristine and vinblastine.

Properties: Stomachic, hypoglycemic, sedative and anti-cancerous.

Forms of use: Decoction of root and leaves, powder.

Medicinal Uses

(a) In Cancer: The plant (violet flowers) is found to be powerful anti-cancerous yielding two important alkaloids vincristine and vinblastine. They are powerful cytotoxic agents which arrest dividing cells in cancer. They are being used to treat Hodgkin's, non-Hodgkin's lymphomas, leukaemia, breast cancer and other related problems.

(b) Other Uses

1. It is also used as hypoglycemic agent (in diabetes).
2. As it is sedative in nature it is often used in stomachache.

3. Annona squamosa Linn.

Family	:	Annonaceae		
Name	:	Hindi	–	Sharifa
		Sanskrit	–	Sitaphal
		English	–	Custard apple
		Bengali	–	Ata

Description: A tree about 20ft high, leaves oblong, lanceolate or elliptic, obtuse or subacute, glaucous, and pubescent beneath when young. Fruit glocose, 2 to 4 inch diameter, tuberculate, yellowish brown, pulp dense. The seeds are many, black, smooth and oblong.

Distribution: All over India, cultivated

Parts used: Leaves, bark, root, seed and fruit.

Phytochemicals: Alkaloids, ascorbic acid, sugars, oil, acrid principle.

Properties: Astringent, tonic, anthelmintic, purgative, duretic and anti-cancerous.

Forms of use: Fruit, root powder, decoction.

Medicinal Uses

(a) In Cancer

1. It is found to have anti-cancerous properties against

human epidermal carcinoma of the Nasopharynx in tissue culture.

2. Ripe fruit bruised and mixed with salt is applied to malignant tumours to hasten suppuration (pus formation) and healing.

(b) Other Uses

1. Leaves made into a paste without adding water are applied to unhealing ulcers.
2. A paste of seeds powder is applied to uterus to cause abortion.
3. Fresh leaves after crushing applied to nostril, cut short fits of hysteria and fainting.

Doses—

Fruit	...	24 to 48 g
Root Powder	...	0.2 to 0.5 g

Other Useful Plants

Camellia sinensis **(Tea)**—It is a curative herb having established antipyretic and diuretic properties. No wonder tea is the most commonly taken drink after water. It is found that common tea consumption can help check cancer but more researches are required to substantiate this claim. Tea is a rich source of antioxidants.

"Basic life processes of the body result in a by product called the free radicals of oxygen. Free radicals and reactive oxygen species (ROS) in the body are derived either from normal, essential or metabolic process or external sources. These are mostly responsible for and hasten the progress of several diseases. Chronic exposure to free redicals can damage DNA, membrane lipids, lipoproteins and functional and structural proteins."

The human body has several inbuilt mechanisms to protect against free redicals and other ROS. These involve systems of enzymes, which are not completely effective. Many fruits and vegetables also help in countering the free redicals.

"Free redical scavengers of antioxidants have been shown to protect against cancer, counter blockages of heart vessels and prevent heart attacks, decrease the risk of cataract and slow the progression of Parkinson's disease," says Mr. Krishnaswamy, Health Information Center, Bangalore.

There is strong logic behind grandma's insistence on consuming fresh fruits and vegetables. But today's diets compromise on their intake. In addition, costs put it out of reach of many.

There is an increasing body of scientific evidence that claims tea is an abundant source of flavonoid antioxidants and thus an important component of a healthy diet. These flavonoid antioxidants effectively stabilise the free electrons. It has been found that tea beverage has greater antioxidant capacity than most fruit and vegetables per serving and is more potent than vitamins C, D and carotenoids.

We will have to learn to drink tea as tea and not as a sweet, syrupy and milky concoction produced by continuously boiling tea leaves, while milk to a certain extent is beneficial, the addition of excess sugar takes away all positive qualities.

More evidence is being churned out regarding the importance of the role of tea antioxidants as "helpful scavengers." It is clear, though, that a combination of antioxidants may in the long run be more effective than large quantities of any single antioxidant.

***Brassica compestris* (Mustard)**—It is a spice used for flavouring and as a source of edible oil has shown beneficial effects in preventing cancer. The protective enzymes can deactivate cancer causing substances. They may also act by functioning as an antioxidant by enhancing tissue levels of protective enzymes in the body. These substances stimulate specifically the levels of gluthione-s-transferases, GST, a group of enzymes which helps to detoxify the harmful agents. This is reported that all plants of this family (crucifarae) have anti-cancerous potential.

***Brassica oleracea* (Cabbage), *Brassica botrytis* (Cauliflower) and *Brassica caulorопа* (Broccoli)**—All belong to crucifarae family have been found to be effective in deactivating the harmful effects of food toxins. The plants of this family are reported to contain benzyl isothiocyanate which invariably have found to inhibit carcinogenesis. Besides, they are also found to contain some indoles, a chemical activating the microsomal mixed function oxidase activity to the point of detoxification of carcinogenic compounds. Those people who smoke much should take great amount of these vegetables to excrete cancer causing tobacco chemicals from the body. Cruciferous vegetables are good source of anti-carcinogens.

***Curcuma longa* (Turmeric)**—Extract of turmeric, an integral part of Indian cooking and diet, helps reduce clinical symptoms and prevented progression of oral cancer in almost all patients tested. The patients were given 500 mg of turmeric extract thrice daily for fifteen days. Some patients responded early and some with delay. The burning sensation in the mouth and other clinical symptoms decreased in almost every case. The extract is well tolerated with no toxic effects on the liver or kidneys and no loss of appetite. The extract was equally effective in three years old oral cancer lesions. i.e., "Submucous fibrosis" in which the mouth opening gets highly contracted and the colour and texture of skin in the mouth changes (oral lenkoplakia, where white patches develop in the mouth) and "Oral Lichen Planus" where mouth becomes sensitive to hot and cold substances.

The first condition, oral submucous fibrosis, is most common in India, and is present in many "Pan Masala" chewers, while the second, oral lenkoplakia, is common in betel quid chewers.

Apart from what has been described above, more plants like *Podophyllum peltatum* (May apple plant) yielded podophyllotoxin found useful in the treatment of testicular cancers. Taxols from *Taxus brevifolia* and *baccata* are found effective against ovarian cancers. A substance called genistein, found in *Foeniculum vulgare* (Soya) weakens the ability of cancer cells to grow faster so they starve and die. *Allium sativum, Withania somnifera, Trichossanthus dioca* (Parval) are also useful in cancer. Other formulations developed with hers like Sariva, Amrita, Bhallataka are found effective in the cancers of uterine, cervical, liver, kidney, leukaemia, breast cancer and brain tumours.

Now-a-days, as said for the prevention of cancer a holistic approach would be, to use carotene/vitamin A, E, C, B-Complex and iron, selenium in everyday vegetables and fruits: turmeric, ginger, garlic (selenium source), onion, broccoli, cauliflower, cabbage, amla, lemon, orange, papaya, mangoes and other dark green vegetables. Infact, natural products promise a great deal where continuous research will slowly but inevitably pay off, and we may reasonably anticipate the day when it will be possible to find a cure to keep malignancy at bay.

Free On-line Cancer Information Service

The Sitaram Bhartiya Institute of Science and Research, New Delhi has started a free on-line information service on all aspects of cancer. All one has to do is dial 6867435 on weekdays, between 9 am and 5 pm. A trained person on the line will answer queries, in Hindi or English. The information can also be sent by mail or e-mail on request free of charge.

The e-mail address is; sbisr@giasdl01. vsnl.net.in

The CIS (Cancer Information Service) provides information on:

- The nature of cancer,
- ways to detect it early,
- lifestyles to adopt to prevent some cancers,
- tests and techniques to diagnose cancer,
- location and the nearest facility offering treatment of cancer,
- management of side-effects,

- availability of medicines and disposables,
- psychological and social support groups in Delhi,
- rehabilitation services, and the like.

Prophylectics against cancer

- Use of cabbage, cauliflower, broccoli and tomatoes in food.
- Use of coloured fruits and vegetables.
- Use of vitamins (A, C, E) and unsaturated fatty acids (Omega acids).
- Use of mustard oil and mustard saag.
- Use of garlic and turmeric.

8

Plant Foods and their Nutritive values

Plants that are used as food and also of value as therapeutic or prophylactic medicines may be termed as nutriceuticals.

Food is needed as fuel (energy) and as raw material for growth and maintenance of the body. Even in adult life most tissues are continuously broken and replaced, and although some of the material can be resynthesised and used again, much of it is lost.

There are three principal foods—protein, fat and carbohydrate. All three can be used as fuel.

Protein and carbohydrate supply the almost same amount of energy i.e., 4 calories/gram. Fat provides 9.3 calories/gram. But whereas fat and carbohydrate can be freely consumed, a good deal of the protein in the diet must be conserved as building material.

In addition to the three basic components, essential substances that can not be synthesised in the body have to be supplied readymade i.e. vitamins (A, C, B-Complex-water soluble and D, K, E- fat soluble) and minerals (Copper, Zinc, Iron, Manganese, Magnesium, Calcium, Selenium).

A balanced diet constitutes all the above substances in the right proportions i.e., protein, carbohydrate, fat, vitamin and minerals.

Malnutrition which happens mostly in children arises due to inadequate unbalanced diet. Most of the children die as they do not get proper food and become victims of fatal infections of lungs, intestine, atrophy etc; even tuberculosis, a common curable disease among adults, is still a serious problem.

People quite unaware of the nutritive value of plants always opt for conventional sources to tackle the malnutrition problems. But fruits and vegetables available in the market do not let any child/adult to fall victim of deficiency diseases, if eaten regularly.

Role of Plants

1. Magnifera indica, Linn.

Family	:	Anarcardiaceae		
Names	:	Hindi	–	Aam
		Sanskrit	–	Aamra
		English	–	Mango

Description: A large evergreen tree 10-14m high with a heavy dome shape crown and a straight stout bole.

Distribution: Throughout India. Cultivated in most parts of the Indian peninsula. It is common in subtropical Himalayas, hills of western and eastern ghats and forests of central India, Orissa, Assam and Andaman Islands.

Parts used: Fruit, seeds, leaves and bark.

Properties: Ripe fruit laxative, diuretic, anti-haemorrhagic, refreshing, restorative, linthotropic, ophthalmic, astringent, anthelmintic and antidiarrheal, anti-syphilitic and tonic.

Forms of use: Mango kernel, juice of ripe mango, unripe small mango (about torch bulb size), pieces of unripe dried mango seed powder and boiled unripe mango etc.

Phytochemicals: Vit A, C, flavones, carotenes, glucosides, sterol, terpene, aromatic acids, essential oil, fatty acids and phenolics.

Minerals, amino acids and Vitamins—contents of Mango fruit

1. Fluorine : 0.3-0.7 ppm dry edible material

2. Iodine : 0.53 ppm dry edible material
3. Calcium : 96 mg%
4. Magnessium : 27.1 mg%
5. Phosphate : 25.0 mg%
6. Ascorbic acid : 16.0 mg/100g
7. Phosphorus : 16.0 mg/100g
8. Iron : 1.3 mg/100g
9. Carotene : 2743 ug/g
(Vitamin A 2309-15589 1.4%)
10. Vitamin B_1 : 0.08 mg/g
11. Vitamin B_2 : 0.09 mg/g
12. Niacin : 0.90 mg/g
13. Methionine and Lysine (Amino acids)

Medicinal Uses

1. It is a powerful nutritive fruit, containing most of all essential substances needed by our body.
2. It contains vitamins and minerals alongwith important chemicals that keep our body fit and fine. So, it is a complete natural food.
3. Its unripe fruit (of about torch bulb size) if used 6 pieces at a time per day for a week clears all stones from kidney. This should be repeated consecuitively for 3 years in mango season.
4. A drink made from boiled unripe mango with salt is a wonderful remedy for heat stroke.
5. Powdered mango seed when taken 3 times a day cures diarrhoea and dysentery.
6. Mango juice is a restorative tonic. It should be taken throughout the season to stay healthy.
7. Dentrifice prepared from mango leaves keeps teeth healthy.

2. Ficus carica Linn.

Family : Moraceae
Names : Bengali, Gujarati, Hindi, Marathi —Anjir

Sanskrit	–	Anjir
English	–	Fig
Telugu	–	Anjuru
Tamil	–	Simaiyatti
Kannada	–	Anjura

Description: A bush or small tree with a cylindrical stem, it grows to a height about 13ft and has an abundance of latex producing ducts. The rich green leaves are scabrous with a pubescent lower surface, they are 3-5 lobed with a cordate base and are borne on a long petiole. The flowers are monoecious, being enclosed in a flashy receptacle known as syconium which changes from green to deep purple as it ripens.

Distribution: All over India.

Parts used: Leaves, root, fruit.

Phytochemicals: Sugars, protein, salts, vitamin A, B, Coumarins and furo-coumarins etc.

Properties: Pectoral belonging to the thorax; applied to therapeutic agents which have good effect in respiratory diseases, laxative, emollient, energy giving, anti-boil, nutritive, tonic.

Forms of use: Its main use is as an edible fruit having high nutritive value. Decoction and poultice.

Medicinal Uses

1. A fig is high in calories and is easy to digest and assimilate. The latex that oozes out of the freshly cut leaves contain chymase (a milky fluid with a coagulant action), lipase, amylase and protease. It also contains a diastasic enzyme which when applied over uncooked meat increases maturation process.
2. It also has an analgesic effect against insect sting and bites.
3. The leaves can be used in decoction form to condition hair.

4. Decoction of the young branches is an excellent pectoral (for respiratory problems).

5. Fig is a highly nutritious fruit. Since it does not contain any fibre, persons recovering from illness are specially advised to take it. It is a wholesome food which is easily digested.

6. It is also effective in removing gravel in the kidney or the bladder and also helps in the removal of the obstruction of the liver and spleen in subacute cases.

7. The fruit is also given as a cure for piles and gout.

8. It is also beneficial in infantile liver, piles and diarrhoea.

9. Above all it is very useful in leucoderma treatment, patients are advised to take a good size of fig 3 times a day for a month and use juice of fresh leaves on the white spots 2/3 times in a day and bedtime. They can also use moistened leaves of chenopodium (Bathu Ka Sag) on the white spots.

3. Luffa acutangula (Linn) Roxb. Var, amara (Roxb) Clarke

Family	:	Cucurbitaceae		
Names	:	Hindi	–	Torai
		Sanskrit	–	Koshataki
		English	–	Ribbed gourd
		Bengali	–	Thinga
		Gujarati	–	Kadavighisodi
		Tamil	–	Peypirakam
		Telugu	–	Aelavibua
		Trade name	–	Kukarvela

Description: A climber, leaves 4 to 8 inch long, orbicular reniform, 5 lobed, flower yellow, stamens 3, strongly ribbed ovary. Fruit 6 to 12 inch long, clavate, oblong obtuse, smooth, longitudinally ribbed. Seed 1/4 to 1/3 inch ovoid-oblong, compressed, black, not winged.

Distribution: Cultivated throughout India.

Parts used: Fruit, seeds, root and leaves.

Properties: Nutritive, bitter tonic, diuretic, demulcent, expectorant and hypoglycemic.

Phytochemicals: Amino acids—arginine, glycine, threonine, glutamic acid leucine, Bitter substances—Cucurbitacins, terpenes and saponins, Vitamins and Minerals—Calcium (18mg), Phosphorus (0.5mg), Iron (33mg), Vitamin B_2 (0.01mg), Niacin (0.01mg), Vitamin C (5mg), Carotene (2.6mg). Presence of fluorine, iodine is also reported.

Forms of use: As vegetable, decoction, juice.

Medicinal Uses

1. It is nutritive plant and used as vegetable.
2. It is a bitter tonic and diuretic.
3. Seeds are emetic and purgative.
4. It is useful in the enlargement of spleen.
5. Leaves are good substitute for ipecacuanaha in dysentery.
6. The leaves or its juice are used as a dressing of sores, inflammed spleen, ringworm, piles, leprosy and bites of insects.
7. Oil of seeds is effective in skin diseases.
8. The root is laxative.

4. Withania somnifera (Linn.) Dunal

Family	:	Solanaceae		
Names	:	Hindi	–	Asgandh
		Sanskrit	–	Ashwagandha
		English	–	Winter Cherry
		Bangali	–	Aaskanda
		Gujarati	–	Asoda
		Kannada	–	Hirimaddina gadde
		Marathi	–	Aaskandha
		Malayalam	–	Ammukivann
		Trade name	–	Nagauri asgandha

Description: A small under shrub upto 1.5 high, stem and branches covered with minute star shaped hairs. Leaves upto 10cm long, ovate, hairy-like branches. Flowers pale green, small about 1 cm long, few flowers borne together in short axillary clusters. Fruit 6 mm diameter, globose, smooth red, enclosed in the inflated and membranous calyx.

Distribution: Found throughout India, cultivated.

Properties: Nutritive, tonic, alterant, aphrodisiac and nervine sedative.

Phytochemicals: Alkaloids, amino acids, sterols and neutral compounds.

Forms of use: Powder, decoction, paste of root and leaves.

Medicinal Uses

1. It enforces fresh energy and vigour in a system worn out owing to any constitutional disease like syphilis and in rheumatic fever.
2. Powdered root is very useful with equal parts of ghee and honey for impotence and seminal debility.
3. As nutrient and health restorative to the pregnant and old people, a decoction of the root is recommended.
4. For glandular swelling fresh green root reduced to paste with heated water is applied to the affected parts.
5. For improving sight, a mixture of this plant powder, liqorice powder and juice of emblic myrobalans is recommended.
6. Removes functional obstruction of body, promotes urination.
7. The antibiotic and antibacterial activity of the roots as well as leaves has recently been confirmed.

5. Amaranthus paniculatus, Linn.

Family	:	Amaranthaceae		
Names	:	Hindi	–	Chaulai, Lal Sag

Description: It is small, herbaceous, annual, leaves alternate, abovate, dotted, upto one inch long, half inch broad, tip pointed. Flowers small, in auxillary clusters. Fruits are ovoid, compressed sac, opening transversely.

Distribution: Common in plains of India.

Chemical Compounds: This vegetable is highly nutritious packed as it is with proteins, carbohydrates, calcium, phosphorus, iron, Vitamin A 2500-11000 I.U. and Vitamin C 173 mg/100g. Seeds contain saponin which is slightly toxic.

Parts used: Leaves, root and seeds.

Properties: Carminative, nutritive, antibiotic, emollient, demulcent, aphrodisiac, antirheumatic.

Forms of use: As vegetable, decoction, poultice, juice mixed with lemon and honey.

Medicinal Uses

1. One should eat it regularly to get rid of Vitamins and mineral deficiency. This can serve as a natural protein, amino acids like leucine, lyaine, cysteine and methionine.
2. Taken at any stage, chaulai is believed to be useful in curing vision defects, respiratory infections and recurrent colds.
3. Extract its juice and mixed with honey the decoction is a wonderful remedy against bronchitis, asthma, emphysema and tuberculosis.
4. For infants, a teaspoonful of the fresh juice with honey makes the baby healthy and strong. This also prevents constipation and eases the teething process.
5. The juice of the plant mixed with a teaspoonful of lemon juice battles against bleeding caused by week gums, nose, lungs and even piles.
6. A decoction of the leaves or roots is given in 1/2 ounce in diarrhoea, leucorrhoea, menorrhagia and impotence. A poultice of the leaves with honey is applied over

inflammed and painful parts.

7. The roots are given in colic gonorrhoea and eczema.

8. The seeds are cooling, demulcent and powerfully aphrodisiac, they are given in leucorrhoea and impotence.

9. The leaves are sweetish, expectorant, vulnerary, antipyretic, emmenagogue, emetic, stop suppuration, useful in biliousness, fleshy tumours, toothache, burning sensations, liver complaints, inflammations, decoction as gargle in stomatitis.

10. Externally it is used as emollient poultice, as an application in ulcerated condition of throat and mouth, as a wash for ulcers and sores.

Ubiquinone: A drug in food

Quinones form a large group of naturally occuring substances with representatives in almost all of the phyla (50% quinones are reported only from Rubiaceae family). Of biological interests are various isoperenoid quinones (ubiquinones) plastoquinones and menaquinones.

Investigations of the process of electron transport in the terminal oxidation system of diverse organisms has led to the discovery of a series of lipid soluble isoperenoid quinones which participate in the multienzyme respiratory complex. The quinones appear to have a definite spatial orientation in the complex and probably function by 'shuttling' electrons between other respiratory co-enzymes. In addition, they play a more direct-role in the process of oxidative phosphorylation.

Ubiquinones (Co-enzyme Q) are widely distributed in nature and with exception of gram-positive bacteria and blue green algae they have been detected in all groups of living organisms (be it a bacteria, fungi plants or animals). All mammals have co-enzyme Q in their bodies; heart, kidney, muscle etc., tissues doing more work like heart contain more CoQ. Besides, vegetables -- Potatoes, spinach, cauliflower, carrots, sweet potatoes and soyabeen etc., rape-seed and sesame oils also contain it but quantities in all these are very low and get destroyed upon heating and cooking (so, their use as raw in forms of salad is recommended). The sub-cellular distribution of the ubiquinones shows them to be localised in the mitochondria in animals and plants and the cell membranes of non-photosynthetic bacteria. The ubiquinones are all derivatives of 5, 6-dimethoxy-3-methyl-2 transpolyprenyls-1, 4-benzo-quinone (where n=1-13) and generally most organisms synthesise a series of ubiquinones, usually those where n=8, 9 or 10 predominate. In human being n=10 so CoQ_{10}. Variations on this structural pattern such as amino substitution in the benzoquinone nucleus and reduction or opoxidation of isolated double bonds in the polyprenyl chain have also been noticed. The liver cells of healthy human beings have the ability to take the CoQ of lower varieties and change into CoQ_{10}. This ability is reduced in sickness and old age and a fall in CoQ_{10} level leads to ill health and a fall of 75% is observed near death.

In our body tissue cells are the building blocks or units by whose continuous work body gets energy and strength and these tiny working units furnish all kinds of compounds as per body needs from the routine meals that we take. The wear and tear of the body (tissues) is also repaired and rejected tissue-parts which are excreted are replaced by new cells and this is a automatic chain process. This total work without any break needs energy. It is also needed for body's involuntary works viz., for heart to beat, for lungs to breath, for brain to think, for kidneys to purify blood, for regulating body temperature etc. Besides, energy is also required for eating, cooking, talking, walking and for various types of other jobs. All this energy is also supplied by the same cells from roughly the same raw materials. The total energy (nearly 95%) is produced by the oxidation of food's hydrogen part into water though its transfer needs a number of concerted steps and these steps are strictly maintained. One of these steps which can not be overlooked needs CoQ.

A fall in blood CoQ_{10} level leads to reduced immunity, impaired repair of tissues and generally slowing down of all processes. It is known that aged or weak people have greater susceptibility to illness whose severity is more than that in younger people. Antibiotics can cure an infection but can not enhance the body's resistance which is due to the immune system. Experiments which include man and animals have proved that CoQ works as a stimulant or catalyst for making the macrophages active (those large cells that destroy the invading bacteria) to enhance the immune system, mainly the lymphocytes which are entrusted with the work of production cum-activation of antibodies. At the same time CoQ protects the cellular membrance from damage.

A sound immune system means a healthier body and long disease-free life. Experimental animals when kept on CoQ therapy appeared healthier, looked younger and retained their healthy looks well with prolonged lives.

The use of CoQ in various cardiac ailments came out with astonishing results. It is much beneficial in conjestive heart, digematative heart disease, angina and arrbythima when given orally with routine therapy as it strengthens the heart. It is a boon to every kind of trouble, it reverses the high blood pressure, helps cure gum ailment, helps to ward off weight, protects against heart attacks, soothes stomach ulcers.

In many countries, Sweden, Denmark, Germany and Japan CoQ_{10} is being sold as a dietary capsules containing 10-30 mg of CoQ_{10} which is a tenth of the dose used clinically.

Spirulina: A nutritious algae

Spirulina is a blue-green algae. It is a helical member of oscillatoriacae (cynophyceae), with very delicate transverse walls, occurs both in fresh and marine water. It is an ancient food. It was reported by Leonard and Compere (1967) that algal cakes, sold at the market of Fort-Lamy, Chad

Republique, Africa were mostly made of Spirulina platensis (Nordst). Gutl., found abundantly in small saline lakes north of lake Chad in east Africa. On chemical analysis it was found to have very high percentage of protein and was suggested that this spirulina might be a promising food source. Malack and kilham (1974) reported the rates of photosynthesis are exceptionally high in these lakes and that spirulina platensis is frequent in them.

This nutritious-medicinal tiny algae is now thought to provide singly a whole range of nutrients ranging from proteins to vitamins (including cynacobalamin) and minerals. Its' protein content, the highest ever reported, ranges between 65-70% and is three times that of soyabean and five times more than meat. It has full range of vitamin B-Complex and is the abundant source of vitamin B_{12} which is essential for combating anaemia. Spirulina is also a good source of beta-carotene, a precursor of vitamin A, having twenty times more carotene than carrots and has high amounts of iron, calcium, phosphorus and trace elements like potassium and magnessium.

Its medicinal values are numerous and actually it is boon to human health, combating protein malnutrition, anaemia and other diseases. The high beta-carotene content finds use in curing glucoma, cataract and night blindness. Improvement in haemoglobin levels and control of diabetes have been reported in developed countries following administration of two to five grams of spirulina per day.

It has also been used as a remedy for pancreatitis, cirrohosis and hepatitis and acts as prophylactic against cancer. The algae tablets are also given to increase lactation in nursing mothers and improve their health and immune system. Spirulina can reduce blood sugar and cholesterol level effectively and improve health of skin.

It helps to control obesity by affecting levels of phenylalanine, an essential amino acid in the body, and thereby suppressing appetite levels. It also contains many polyunsaturated fatty acids which help to reduce cholesterol level in the body on long term basis (ten grams of plant introduce thirteen mg of cholesterol in the blood and provide 36 calories of energy).

Cosmetics preparations of algae rich in vitamin E have been found to improve the skin health. When applied on cuts/wounds they help in quick healing by promoting cell regeneration.

The algae is cultivated by allowing to boom in sunlight in a suitable pond containing alkaline water and harvested using some efficient technique involving membrane filters etc. The Central Food Technological Research Institute, Mysore is working on this product and it has been launched as a health food-cum-drug.

9

Disturbed Menses and related Problems

Menstruation

Periodic (monthly) bleeding in women of child bearing age (menses). When a girl is born her ovaries contain the rudiments of upto half a million eggs (ova), which lie dormant until puberty. From then until the menopause (a condition wherein menstruation stops in women, normally at around 45 years of age) some 30 years later, an ovum is released each month from one or other ovary (ovulation), and finds its way to the adjacent fallopian tube. Before it is released an ovum ripens in a sort of shell, the Graafian follicle. Only the ovum, a single cell, is released. The follicle remains in the ovary and grows into a small endocrine gland, corpus-luteum.

The corpus-luteum produces a hormone, progesterone, that stimulates the lining of the uterus to form a thick layer, with an abundant circulation of blood, ready to receive an embryo if the ovum becomes fertilized.

An embryo forms a hormone that keeps the corpus luteum in being and so preserves the enriched lining of the uterus. But if the ovum is not fertilized, the corpus luteum withers in two weeks time, and the uterus, deprived of progesterone, sheds its lining. The process is spread over a few days. The raw surface left behind bleeds a little, the average loss during a menstrual period is about 60ml of blood (excessive bleeding with menstruation is called menorrhagia).

As soon as bleeding is over the lining of the uterus

regenerates, and some two weeks later the cycle begins again with the release of another ovum.

The interval between ovulation and menstruation i.e., the life span of the corpus-luteum if there is no pregnancy-is nearly always two weeks. But the interval between menstruation and next ovulation varies from person to person, and also from month to month in same person. The whole cycle may last three weeks time or more.

Dysmenorrhoea

Pain with menstrual periods, mainly in the lower abdomen or the small back. Secondary (symptomatic) dysmenorrhoea in women who have previously had normal periods can arise from a whole range of gynaecological disorders, and is treated by identifying and dealing with the cause.

The most common disorder is primary dysmenorrhoea, affecting girls from their first period or soon after. Neither the cause nor even the source of the pain is known, although this must be the commonest ailment (except perhaps acne) of adolescent girls and young women. Pain at the start of a period is vaguely ascribed to reduction of blood flow by spasms of the uterus (a sort of anginal pain) and pain that comes on later due to congestion, and it is true that the early types of dysmenorrhoea are sometimes relieved by drugs that relax spasm, and the later type by lying down, which may help to prevent blood from gravitating to the pelvis. Many cases respond to treatment with hormones, especially those that prevent ovulation (the contraceptive pills). This strongly suggests defective balance of sex hormones as an underlying cause.

Severe primary dysmenorrhoea can be incapacitating at the height of the attack but it does not lead to any worse trouble, and its tendency is to gradually become better. A few cases persist after the birth of the first child, and some improve after marriage but before pregnancy. This could be an agreement in favour of a hormonal cause or as some people believe, of an emotional cause. In fact, it could be either or both, because the production of hormones and the emotional state are inextricably tangled. Considering that emotional disturbances can completely stop menstrual periods it would not be surprising if it contributes to painful periods.

Although the pain certainly has a physical basis, the amount of distress it causes may depend on emotional factors. Anything to do with sex is emotionally charged, and if dysmenorrhoea is commoner and more severe in our society than other, our social taboos and religious teachings may well be to blame.

Amenorrhoea

Absence of menstrual periods. Literally, the term includes the state of girls before puberty and women after the menopause, but it is more sensibly confined to women of child bearing age who do not menstruate. Primary amenorrhoea means that menstruation has never begun; perhaps the most important point here is that some girls start late; but each case needs full investigation becuase some defect of structure or hormone balance may need attention.

Secondary amenorrhoea means that the patient who has previously had periods has stopped having them. The obvious and usual reasons are pregnancy and the menopause (which can be unexpectedly early). Otherwise, the condition can be a symptom of all kinds of illness, including emotional upsets.

Amenorrhoea is not an illness but a symptom, and it is harmful in itself only because the feeling that she is not behaving normally disturbs the patient. Menses usually start at the age of 12 to 16 years, depending upon the climatic conditions and stops at the age of 40-45 years.

Leucorrhoea

Excess of white or colourless secretion from the vagina. It

may be only an exaggeration of the normal secretion, or a symptom of irritation anywhere in the genital organs, such as the common infections with trichomonas or candida.

Treatment

A number of plants are found useful in the treatment and management of above diseases. Apart from their use, diet control, excercise and meditation is also necessary.

Role of Plants

1. Saraca indica, Linn.

Family	:	Caesalpiniaceae		
Name	:	Hindi	–	Angana priya
		Sanskrit	–	Asoka
		English	–	Asoka Tree
		Gujarati	–	Ashoka
		Kannada	–	Asokadamara
		Malayalam	–	Vanjulam
		Tamil	–	Asogam
		Trade name	–	Ashoka

Description: A small tree, leaves compound, evergreen, forming a dense crown, leaflets 7-25 cm long, slightly leathery. Flowers bright orange coloured due to coloured bracts in small dense bunches. Fruits 15-25 cm long, flat, seeds many.

Distribution: It is cultivated almost throughout India especially in eastern and south India.

Parts used: Stem, bark, flower and seeds.

Phytochemicals: Tannin, catechin, sterol, saponin, glycoside and an organic compound with iron.

Properties: Astringent, sedative, uterine stimulator.

Forms of use: Decoction, powder, syrup, paste.

Medicinal uses

(a) (i) In menses—It acts directly on the muscular fibres of the uterus and has stimulating effect on the ovarian tissues. So, it is used in the treatment of menorrhagia and allied diseases.

(ii) Extracts of the plant are considered important to treat disturbed menstrual cycle.

(iii) Asoka bark is very useful in uterine affections especially in menses.

(b) Other uses

Bark is useful in internal bleeding, haemorrhoids and blood dysentery.

Doses—

Decoction	...	28 to 112 ml.
Powder	...	1 to 3 g.

2. Sida cordifolia Linn

Family	:	Malvaceae		
Names	:	Hindi	–	Kharenti
		Sanskrit	–	Jayanti
		English	–	Country mallow
		Bangali	–	Beelelaa
		Gujarati	–	Baldaana
		Kannada	–	Kisangee
		Marathi	–	Chiknaa
		Tamil	–	Paniyaar-tutthi
		Trade name	–	Kharenti, Nilatutthi

Description: A small, much-branched shrub, minute star shaped hair present all over the plant, leaves 2-5 cm, ovate or roundish, thick, margine toothed petioles shorter than leaves. Flowers, yellow, small, one or a few together, fruits 6-8 mm diameter, divided into 7-10 parts, each strongly retionlated, and with two spiny projections on tip.

Distribution: The plant occurs throughout India, as a common weed usually on waste places and open scrub forests.

Parts used: Root, leaves and seeds.

Phytochemicals: Alkaloid, sterol and glucosides.

Properties: Cooling, astringent, stomachic, tonic, aromatic, bitter, febrifuge, demulcent, diurectic and anti-menorrhagia/leucorrhoea.

Forms of use: Powder, decoction, root infusion.

Medicinal Uses

(a) It is very useful in womens' diseases like menorrhagia and leucorrhoea with sedative action.

(b) **Other Uses**

(i) The juice of the plant is given in rheumatism, gonorrhea and spermatorrhea.

(ii) Roots are given in urinary diseases and disorder of blood and bile.

(iii) Also useful in bleeding piles, haemeturria, cystitis, blood dysentery, nervous diseases, paralysis, asthma and is a cardio-tonic.

3. Abroma augusta (Linn.)

Family	:	Sterculiaceae		
Names	:	Hindi, Bengali	—	Olat kambal
		Sanskrit	—	Pinchaskarpas
		English	—	Devil's cotton.

Description: Root is browinsh in colour, fibrous, and has distinct odour. Root bark has a dull brown outer surface which is longitudinally wrinkled alongwith small lenticels. The inner surface is smooth, dark brown and longitudinally striated. Bark is not brittle and can be easily separated.

Distribution: Grown throughout the hotter parts of India. It is also cultivated for its showy, deep scarlet flowers.

Parts used: Root, root bark, stem, leaves.

Properties: Leaves and stem are demulcent, root bark is an emmenagogue. It is reported as oxytocic and liable to produce dermatitis, anti-dysmenorrhea.

Phytochemicals: Alkaloids, sterols.

Forms of use: Powder, decoction, leaf-infusion.

Medicinal Uses

(a) **In menses**—Fresh juice of the root bark is more efficacious and given in dysmenorrhea. A single administration during the menses will regulate the menstrual flow.

(b) **Other Uses**

(i) Infusion in cold water of fresh leaves and stem is very useful in gonorrhea.

(ii) Also acts as a uterine tonic and to facilitate conceptions in young married women.

Doses:	Root, bark	... 1 to 2 g
	Decoction of root	... 14 to 50 ml
	Leaf infusion	... 15 to 25 ml

Other Useful Plants

- ***Crocus sativus* (Kesar)**—It is a popular remedy for promoting menstruation generally in fever, hysteria, meloncholia, leukorrhea and piles.
- ***Datura metal* (Dhatura safed)**—The liniment obtained by cooking 28g seeds of Dhatura safed in any bland oil is useful in relieving pain in difficult menstruation and in some painful affections of the uterus.
- ***Erythrina variegata* (Feraud)**—Leaf juice is said to have cured long standing dysmenorrhea, and also removed sterility in fatty women by gradually reducing fat and producing natural menstrual flow.
- ***Aritolochia bracteata* (Kiromari)**—In small doses it promotes digestion and regulates menstruation.
- ***Mucuna pruriens* (Kuwanch)**—Seeds are very useful in profuse menstruation and leukorrhea etc.
- ***Ricinus comunis* (Redy)**—A poultice of leaves are applied over the pubic region of women to promote menstrual flow.

- **Artemesia nilgaris (Nagaduna)**—Prescribed in obstructed menses, hysteria and preventing abortion in form of infusion.
- ***Bahunia Variegata*** **(Godhaparna)**—Decoction of buds used in menorrhagia.
- ***Nardostachip grandiflora*** **(Jathamansi)**—It is also used as laxative and for improving urination, menstruation and digestion.
- ***Penganum harmala*** **(Harmal)**—Seeds are used to regulate menstruation.
- ***Perguleria daemia*** **(Utran)**—It is also used in profuse menstruation.
- ***Symplocos cacemosa*** **(Lodh)**—It is an astringent and is used in excessive bleeding during menstruation.
- ***Hemidesmus indicus*** **(Anantmul)**—It is useful in leucorrhoea and urinary complaints.
- ***Acacia catechu*** **(Kaththa)**—Useful in bleeding piles, uterine haemorrhage and leucorrhoea.

In most cases attention to general health will bring about relief in such cases. Regular exercise is of value in stimulating the blood circulation. Anaemia and constipation should receive proper treatment.

Medicines

Ayurvedic	:	Ashokarist, Lukol
Unani	:	Supari-pak
Homoepathic	:	Pulsatilla complex

10
Mental Diseases

The nervous system enables us to move, to be aware of things, and to collect our impressions together. From all we have remembered we then make decisions and perform work, whether it is the handling of implements or the creation of art or music. The same nervous system provides us with simple and primitive reflexes and also enables us to avoid being bound by reflex action reactions. It controls our bodies, our glands, breathing, heart, bowels, and bladder. It makes us stay awake or makes us sleep, and when we sleep it makes us dream. When the nervous system is upset, we get pins and needles in the finger-tips, numbness, paralysis, epilepsy and migraine etc.

The nervous system explains the whole field of nerves. It covers subjects as diverse as memory, how the brain affects behaviour, how we see, hear, smell, balance, imagine, how messages are sent along the nerves, and how the nervous system has some resemblance to computers.

The part of the control nervous system is enclosed by the skull. Like its continuation the spinal cord, the brain starts life as a simple tube. But whereas the spinal cord retains this form throughout life, the brain grows into a complex system of bulges and folds.

At an early stage of embryonic life, three bulbous dwellings appear at the front end of the tube that is to form the central nervous system, and these develop into the three main divisions of the brain: hindbrain, midbrain and forebrain.

The original tube is still recognizable in the adult brain as the brain-stem, seen as an extension into the skull of the spinal cord. It is a central core from which the larger portions of the brain (cerebellum and cerebrum) grow.

Very roughly speaking, the further from the spinal cord the more advanced the function, progressing from reflexes for maintaining vital functions such as the circulation of blood and breathing in the lower part of the hindbrain to the processes of intelligent behaviour in the outer layers of the forebrain. But structure and function are only loosely related, for the whole nervous system works as an integrated unit.

Hindbrain: The spinal cord continues into the skull as the medulla oblongata. In the cord, the nerve cells form a fluted rod (grey matter) surrounded by nerve fibres (white matter). In the medulla the grey matter is gathered into more or less distinct groups of cells or nuclei; this tendency increases further up the brain. These nuclei include the cells of several cranial nerves and also the vital centres which regulate fundamental activities such as the heartbeat.

Above the medulla oblongata is a large, rounded, backward projection, the cerebellum. It fills the posterior fossa of the skull, i.e., the part immediately above the nape of the neck. The cerebellum governs many reflex actions such as balance and posture. At the same level, the pons is a broad band across the front of the brain-stem, like a strap to hold the cerebellum in place.

Midbrain: Above the pons the brain-stem resumes its primitive tubular structure. The midbrain is a short cylinder from which the stalks of the two cerebral hemispheres (forebrain) arise. It contains the cells of some cranial nerves, relay stations for the senses of sight and hearing, and centres for the coordination of movements. The reticular formation is a criss-cross arrangement of grey and white matter. It can be traced through the whole length of the brain-stem but is most obvious in the centre of the midbrain. It appears to act as a central switchboard for the whole brain.

Forebrain: Above the midbrain the brain-stem bends sharply forward, and the narrow central canal widens to a deep vertical cleft, the third ventricle. At each side of the ventricle is a mass of grey matter the thalamus. Sensations of all kinds are received here and distributed to reflex pathways or to the cerebral cortex and consciousness. Crude sensation, particularly pain is perceived in the thalamus itself. Below is the hypothalamus, the highest centre of the automatic nervous system, from which is suspended the pituitary gland (it is a typical endocrine gland, composed of hormone secreting cells of several kinds). Behind is a small protrusion, the pineal body (a small bulb like profusion from the centre of the brain, its function in man is not known). The whole complex, representing the headward end of the brain stem, is sometimes called tween-brain.

Projecting from either side of the tween-brain and completely enclosing it are the relatively huge cerebral hemispheres, which make up the greater part of the human brain. It is only through the development of the cerebral hemispheres that a man's brain is relatively longer than a monkey's or a monkey's than a dog's. An elephant's brain is four times larger than man but in relation to the size of the animal it is much smaller.

The central cavity of a cerebral hemisphere, the lateral ventricle, opens by a narrow isthmus (for a man of Monro) into a third ventricle. It is surrounded by masses of grey matter, the basal ganglia, which are concerned with muscle action immediately below the level of consciousness. Disorders of the basal ganglia cause Parkinsonism—shaking palsy. The surface of the hemispheres is covered with a layer of grey matter, the cerebral cortex. Between the cortex and the underlying basal ganglia and thalamus is a brand zone of white matter, composed of nerve fibres to and from the cells of the cortex.

Definite functions can be ascribed to certain areas of the cerebral cortex. The areas for voluntary movement and for most types of sensation have been plotted in detail. But no particular area can be alloted to such functions as reason or memory.

Nervous tissue needs a large and constant supply of oxygen and glucose, walking or sleeping, thinking or idling. It ceases to work after few seconds if the supply is cut off, and irreparable damage is done in a few minutes. The rate of circulation in other organs varies widely but the brain receives about 750 cc of blood/minute, by the carotid and vertebral arteries, regardless of what is going on elsewhere. The complicated mechanisms for maintaining the blood pressure are mainly to keep up this supply.

The brain is enclosed by fibrous membranes, the meninges, and by the cerebrospinal fluid.

The behaviour of nervous tissue, of which brain is composed, is being discussed as even the simplest animal—a protozoan made of a single cell—responds to a stimulus by withdrawing itself. In more advanced creatures some of the cells in the outer layer of the body are adopted to receive stimulae and transmit them to other cells adopted for movement. Cells that transmit impulses to other cells are called nerve cells or neurons. In all higher animals the neurons are gathered together to from an anatomical unit, the nervous system, derived entirely from the outermost layer of the embryo (ectoderm), which also forms the outer coat of the skin.

In the embryo of a vertebrate (such as man) the future neurones are gathered in the midline of the surface of the back. This strip running the length of the embryo is first depressed to form a groove and then submerged, as the tissues of the back close over it, to from tube. Later this neural tube is surrounded by the skull and vertebrae to form brain and spinal cord, together making central nervous system which largely functions through reflex action (i.e., involuntarily).

In all vertebrates a special system of nerves regulates the organs of blood-circulation, respiration, digestion, excretion and reproduction. Since its activity is wholly reflex and appears to be independent of the brain, that's why it is called autonomic system.

Two kinds of mechanisms control body functions: nervous activity and chemical activity through hormones released from glands such as pituitary and thyroid. The difference between a nerve and a gland is that a nerve releases its chemical transmitter at a given point, where it is destroyed as soon as it has acted, whereas a gland releases its transmitter into blood stream to act throughout the body.

A nerve cell returns to its resting state almost immediately after transmitting an impulse, within one or two milliseconds, its charge, restored and ready to be fired again. The process can be repeated indefinitely. Walking or sleeping, the nervous system is constantly active throughout life. No fresh cells, it seems, are formed after birth. The original stock serves for a lifetime, and the cells that wear out and die are not replaced.

Disorders

Memory is a state where one can remember the past. Mental illness are presumably disturbances of the brain but this is open to dispute because nobody can say where or what the mind is. Some of the disorders are: Anxiety, depression, insomnia, neurasthenia, schizophrenia, hysteria and vertigo-giddiness.

Anxiety: The most common problem in today's fast life. In a biological sense, anxiety is the same as fear. It is the normal response of the body to recognized danger where numerous reflexes are involved, supply of blood to the muscles increases, heart beats more rapidly partly because the blood vessels of the muscles dialate while other organs constrict, diverting the flow where needed more. The muscles themselves are tensed, breathing is deeper and more quick. Urination is increased and there is loss of appetite.

Insomnia (Sleeplessness): One should sleep atleast 6-8 hours and children more. It is essential as during sleep body relaxes, repairing of wear and tear of the body is done. Insomnia is a very common symptom. It can be a direct result of physical symptom such as pain, itching or indigestion. Anxiety makes it difficult to go to sleep, and depression causes early waking. Sometimes heart disease, high blood pressure, kidney and liver disorders produce severe pain and may cause sleeplessness.

Hysteria: A kind of neurosis, most often affecting women and once thought to arise in the uterus. Sustained anxiety, worries, causes it.

Epilepsy: An ill defined group of disorders characterized by fits. A fit is an episode of disorganized and excessive activity in some part of the brain, causing fits, twitching of body muscles, frothing of saliva from mouth and clinching of teeth. Correct cause is not known but head injury and fever etc., can cause it.

Schizophrenia: A kind of psychosis or mental derangement, caused by a series of mental symptoms. The correct cause is unknown.

In all these diseases apart from medicine, psychological treatment plays more positive role and patient is alright after sometime.

Treatment

Plants also play effective role in mental diseases and thus strengthening human nervous system.

Role of Plants

1. Evolvulus alsinoides Linn.

Family	:	Convolvulaceae		
Names	:	Hindi	–	Shankapushpi
		Sanskrit	–	Vishnukranti
		English	–	
		Bengali	–	Shankapushpi
		Gujarati	–	Shankhavala
		Trade name	–	Shankhapushpi

Description: A perennial herb with small woody branches, stems, numerous leaves, 6-20 by 4-8mm, elliptic, oblong, obtuse, acute at base, flowers-light blue, seeds in usually 4, glabrous.

Distribution: A plant growing as a common weed in open and grassy places throughout India, ascending upto 6000 ft. in the Himalayas.

Parts used: The whole herb.

Properties: Bitter tonic alterant, febrifiye, anthelmintic and brain tonic.

Phytochemicals: Alkaloids, sterols, protein, amino acids, carbohydrates, phenolic compounds and tanins.

Forms of use: Decoction, powder, infusion.

Medicinal Uses

As brain tonic—the whole plant in the form of decoction or infusion is used in loss of memory in doses of 56 to 112 ml.

Other Uses

1. Its decoction is also used in fever, nervous debility and epilepsy.
2. It is a good remedy in bowel complaints-dysentery.
3. In diarrhoea/indigestion, a decoction with Tulsi leaves is very useful.
4. In bronchitis/asthma, its leaves are made into cigarettes and smoked.
5. It is also used as anthelmintic.
6. It increases appetite.
7. It brightens the intellect.
8. It improves complexion.
9. It strengthens the brain and memory.
10. When used on scalp, promotes hair growth.

2. Bacopa Monnieri Linn-Pennell

Family : Schrophulariaceae
Name : Hindi – Brahmi
Sanskrit – Saumyalata

English	–	Indian pennywart
Bengali	–	Brahmishaak
Gujarati	–	Nirbrahmi
Tamil	–	Nirbrahmi
Trade name	–	Jalnim

Description: This herb spreads on ground and its stems and small leaves are succulent, i.e., fleshy. Roots arise on the nodes of the stem also. Flowers arise in the axils of the leaves and are borne on short pedicels. One of the five sepals is larger than others. The corolla is bluish-white in colour and about 1 cm across.

Distribution: This herb is found in moist or wet places, such as on borders of water channels, wells, irrigated fields, etc. in all parts of India.

Parts used: Whole plant.

Properties: Brain tonic, diuretic and cardio-tonic.

Phytochemicals: Alkaloids, Mannitol, saponin, sterols.

Forms of use: Infusion, powder, decoction

Medicinal Uses

As brain-tonic, enhancing power of speech and arresting processes of aging and overcoming stress. It is valued in medicine as a tonic for nerves and is prescribed in nervous disorders (accompanied by convulsions or unconsciousness), mental diseases, epilepsy, insanity, neuresthenia, and hysteria.

Other Uses

1. It is also used in constipation and in urinary diseases.
2. Leaf juice is given to infants in bronchitis.
3. Leaf juice mixed with petroleum jelly is applied in rheumatism.
4. The plant is considered as blood purifier.
5. It is also a cardio tonic.
6. A poultice made of the boiled plant is placed on the

chest in acute bronchitis and other coughs in children.

3. Acorus calamus, Linn

Family	:	Araceae		
Names	:	Hindi	—	Gharbacha
		Sanskrit	—	Bhuta-nashini
		English	—	Sweet Flag
		Bengali	—	Bacha
		Gujarati	—	Vaj
		Kannada	—	Baje
		Malayalam	—	Vashanpa
		Marathi	—	Vekhanda
		Trade name	—	Bacha

Description: A herb with long, creeping-branched aromatic rhizomes. Flowering shoots supported by a large leaf like structure called spathe. Flowers small, pale green, in 5-10cm long, cylinderical spikes called spadix; fruits yellow.

Distribution: Almost throughout India, also cultivated.

Parts used: Rhizome.

Properties: Aromatic, bitter, brain tonic, carminative, diuretic, aphrodisiac, tranquillizer.

Phytochemicals: Alkaloid, terpenes, glycoside, aromatic volatile oil.

Forms of use: As powder, infusion, tincture, fluid extract.

Medicinal uses: In mental diseases. The oil from rhizome is a good nerve stimulant and the essential oil free alcoholic extract shows marked sedation and analgesic (pain-soothing) properties justifying its use in mental diseases.

Other Uses

1. Its infusion is given in diarrhoea, dysentery, bronchial and chest diseases and epilepsy.
2. It is considered a household remedy for flatulent colic.
3. Its poultice is used in rheumatic swellings.

Other Useful Plants

Blepharis edulis (Utanjan), ***Rowalfia serpentina*** (Sarpgandha), ***Centella asiatica*** (Mandukaparni), ***Withania somnifera*** (Ashwagandha), ***Nardostachys jatamansi*** (Jatamansi), ***Valeriana wallichi*** (Tagara), ***Celastrus paniculatus*** (Jyotishmati) and ***Emblica officinalis*** (Amla).

Medicines

Ayurvedic	:	Mentat syrup
	:	Alert capsule
	:	Brain Tablet
Unani	:	Khamira Aberasham
	:	Khamira Abaresham Jawahar wala
	:	Dimaghin
Homoeopathic	:	Kali Phos
	:	Five Phos
	:	Strychnium Complex

11

Skin Diseases

The two principal layers of the skin are the dermis, composed of tough, elastic connective tissue with a rich network of blood vessels and nerves and the epidermis, a protective outer layer without blood vessels. The epidermis has a deep layer of growing cells and a covering of dried, dead cells that are constantly shed and replaced by growing layer.

The sweat glands are curled tubes of epidermis that grow down into the dermis. The nails and hair are also derived from epidermis. Like sweat glands, hair follicle give rise to a few grease glands.

The skin is more than a waterproof jacket for the body. It is an active and versatile organ of sensation and adaptation to the dynamic environment.

Since it is almost waterproof, the skin prevents rapid absorption or evaporation at the surface of the body and so helps to keep the amount of water in the body constant. It is a fairly good shield against injury-after all, it is leather-and it heals quickly if it is damaged, unless a large area is lost. Sweat and sebum are both mildly antiseptic in nature.

The sensation of touch, pressure, warmth, cold and pain provide much information about the environment and provide warning of certain dangers. Sometimes by evoking protective reflexes.

The most elaborate function of the skin is to keep the internal temperature of the body constant.

Disorders

Hundreds of different skin diseases have been described.

Many are analogous with diseases of other organs. The skin suffers for more injuries than the rest of the body, and although it is a fairly good barrier to infection it is so much exposed that many types of infections are common. They include virus infections (e.g., warts), bacterial infections (boils, impetigo) and fungal infections (ringworm) and also infestation with larger parasites such as scabies. Fleas and lice can be dangerous because they transmit infectious diseases.

Ringworm: One of the commonest skin diseases; it is an infection of the outer layer of the skin with a microscopical fungus or mould, with certain types the infection tends to spread outwards as a disc; the centre heals while the circumference is still active, forming a ring.

Common sites are the scalp (true "ringworm"), the groin ("dhobie itch") and between the toes ("athlete's foot").

Itching is common to all forms, with ringworm of the scalp, small patches of hair are temporarily lost. The nails of the fingers or toes may harbour the fungus and become deformed, often in association with athlete's foot.

Impetigo: Infection of the outer layers of the skin by staphylococci, forming clusters of small abscesses. It is contagious, especially among children, and from the original site other areas of the patient's own skin can be infected by contact.

Scabies (the itch): A minor but distressing disease caused by a tiny insect, the itch-mite (Sarcoptes scabei), of which the female burrows just under the surface of the skin to lay eggs. The usual sites are soft moist skin, as in front of the elbows or in the groins. The main symptom is itching which may be complicated by infection of scratch marks with bacteria.

Allergy: Allergy and irritation by noxious substances cause many kinds of dermatitis (eczema). They are the commonest of all occupational diseases.

Because it is open to inspection the skin often shows

signs of illness of the body as a whole e.g., the rashes of many fevers or the skin changes of vitamin deficiencies.

The skin has more unexplained diseases than other organs, perhaps because disorders that would be too slight to arouse comment in any other organ are enough to irritate the skin and—which is more important—arouse a sense of disgust. Acne, for instance, brings great distress to adolescents, yet in purely physical terms it is hardly worth calling a disease. Even psoriasis, which most people would regard as a fairly serious skin disease, may be no more than a rather unusual response to some form of irritation.

Plants also play important role in combating skin diseases like: Eczema, Leucoderma, Psoriasis, Urticaria, Ringworm, Dandruff etc.

Role of Plants

1. Lawsonia inermis, Linn.

Family	:	Lythraceae		
Name	:	Hindi+Beng.	–	Mehndi
		Kannada	–	Mayilanchi
		Sanskrit	–	Mendika
		English	–	Henna
		Tamil	–	Marithonali
		Marathi	–	Mendhi
		Gujarati	–	Medi, mendi
		Telugu	–	Goranti

Description: A medium sized much branched shrub. Leaves opposite, 2-3 cm long, often sharp pointed. Flowers small, white fragrant, fruit small, size of small pea, round, seeds many.

Distribution: Throughout India, cultivated.

Parts used: Leaves, fruit, bark, root.

Properties: Aromatic, antifungal, anti-bacterial, cooling, astringent.

Phytochemicals: Phenols, glycosides, anthraquiones etc.

Forms of use: Paste, decoction, powder.

Medicinal Uses

(a) Skin diseases: The leaves of the plant are used as a prophylactic against skin diseases. Its paste is applied on the affected part. It is also antifungal in action, so if paste is applied on nails or affected part continuously for fifteen days cure fungal infection. Avoid extra indulgence in water.

(b) Other Uses

1. The paste of leaves is largely used in Indian homes in headache, burning sensation in feet.
2. Its powder is applied locally on boils and burns.
3. A decoction of leaves is used as gargle in sore throat.
4. The leaves have also shown to have some action against tubercular and other bacterial and in typhoid and haemorrhagia.
5. It is a natural hair dye.

2. Azadirachta indica, A. Juss.

Family	:	Meliaceae		
Names	:	Hindi	–	Neem
		Sanskrit	–	Nimba
		English	–	Persian lilac
		Malayalam	–	Veppa bijam
		Tamil	–	Veppu virat
		Gujarati	–	Limado nu bij
		Kannada	–	Bevinamara bija
		Marathi	–	Kadunimba cha Bi
		Trade name	–	Neem bija

Description: Neem is a very well known tree of India. The tree has pinnate leaves. Flowers small, white fragrant, in short axillary bunches. Fruits 1.2 - 1.8 cm long, green, yellow, seed one in each fruit.

Distribution: All over India.

Parts used: Root bark, fruit, seeds, leaves, flowers, bark, gum etc.

Properties: Anthelmintic, antiseptic, bitter deodorant, diuretic, febrifuge, insecticidal, insect repellent, antiviral and anti-bacterial.

Phytochemicals: Flavone glycosides, sterols, terpenes, alkaloids, bitter compounds and oils.

Forms of use: As paste, decoction, infusion, ointment.

Medicinal Uses

(a) Skin diseases

1. The leaves are bitter and are largely applied on skin diseases and boils.
2. Paste of neem bark is also applied on skin boils for quick healing.
3. Ripe fruits of neem are eaten to get rid of skin diseases.
4. Decoction of leaves is also used for washing wounds.
5. Decoction of flowers is often used for washing wounds.
6. The antibiotic activity of roots of the tree and their utility in skin diseases have been confirmed experimentally.

(b) Other uses

1. The bark is bitter tonic, astringent and antiperiodic i.e., it is useful in fevers, it breaks the periodic sequence of fevers (like malaria) and is useful in skin diseases.
2. Decoction of flowers is also given for blood purification.
3. Oil is useful in leprosy, ulcers etc.
4. Decoction of leaves is used for washing aching ears and eyes.
5. Leaves are powerful insecticide.

3. Psoralea corylifolia, Linn

Family	:	Fabaceae		
Names	:	Hindi	–	Babchi
		Sanskrit	–	Sugandh kantak
		English	–	Psoralea
		Marathi	–	Bavachya
		Tamil	–	Kaarpokarishi
		Telugu	–	Bhaavanchi vittulu
		Bengali	–	Bakuchidaanaa
		Gujarati	–	Baabchi
		Kannada	–	Bavanchigidda
		Malayalam	–	Karpokkart
		Trade name	–	Baabchi

Description: It is an erect herb with densely gland-dotted branches. Leaves round, dotted with black glands on both surfaces. Flowers small, bluish purple, 10-30 in a bunch, arising in axils of leaves. Fruits black, roundish or oblong, closely pitted, seed one, smooth.

Distribution: All over India as a weed in waste places; It is also cultivated.

Parts used: Fruits, leaves and seeds.

Properties: Laxative, anthelmintic, diuretic, oil powerful against skin diseases.

Phytochemical: Coumarins, flavones, terpenes.

Forms of use: Seed oil and extract.

Medicinal Uses

1. The seeds contain an essential oil which is very effective on certain bacteria causing skin diseases. The drug is, therefore, useful in leucoderma and leprosy as an external application as ointment and taken internally.
2. The oleoresinous extracts of the seeds are useful for local application on leucoderma of monsyphilitic origin.
3. Oil shows a moderate antifungal activity.

Other Uses

1. The seeds are also useful for promoting urination and as anthelmintic.

2. Roots of the plant are reported to be useful in caries of teeth and the leaves in diarrhoea.

Doses—

Powder	...	1 to 3 g
Oil	...	External use

Other Useful Plants

1. *Mallotus philipensis* **(Kamela)**—An ointment made of kamela seeds with some bland oil is used for ringworm, scabies, herpes, and other parasitic skin diseases and its powder is given internally to relieve laprous eruptions. Kamela powder (of seeds) alone is applied over syphilitic ulcers.

2. *Curcuma longa* **(Haldi)**—Turmeric powder alone or combined with the pulp of neem leaves is used in ringworms, obstinate itching, eczema, and other parasitic skin diseases.

3. *Allium sativum* **(Lahsun)**—The juice is used as a rubefacient in skin diseases—ringworm and eczema.

4. *Calophyllum inophyllum* **(Champa)**—Leaf juice provide relief in scabies and other skin diseases.

5. *Clerodendrum infortunatum* **(Bhant)**—The stem and root are used externally for tumours and certain skin diseases.

6. *Cuscuta reflexa* **(Akasbel)**—Its juice is used against itch and other skin diseases.

7. *Matricaria chamomilla* **(German Chameli)**—An ointment prepared from it proved to have powerful healing properties and used against various skin infections and boils.

8. *Urginea indica* **(Jangli piyaz)**—Bulb juice is used against leprosy and skin diseases.

9. *Solanum nigrum* **(Makoi)**—The plant juice is used in chronic skin diseases.

10. *Hydnocarous kurzii* **(chalmogra)**—Its oil is used in treatment of leprosy.

11. *Plumbago zeylanica* **(Chitra)**—It is effective in some cases of leucoderma and skin diseases.

12. *Swertia chirata* **(Chiraita)**—It is well reputed drug for skin diseases, it is taken internally to keep away blood disorders.

13. *Argyacia speciosa* **(Samudra shokha)**—The leaves are antiphlogistic, applied over skin diseases and wounds.

Medicines

Ayurvedic	:	Kamillosan ointment
	:	Mahamarichyadi Taila
	:	Somraji Taila (Leprosy)
Unani	:	Marham abyaz
	:	Marham kuba
	:	Majoon Ushba (Syphilis)
Homoeopathic	:	Echinacea complex (Skin diseases)
	:	Cascarea complex
	:	Euphorbia complex (Eczema)

12

Rheumatic Diseases

Arthritis: Inflammation and tissue damage in the joints. The term has been applied to many types of joint diseases, not always correctly because with some types there is no real inflammation. The common factors are pain, occasional-dull-ache, sharp pain and walking painful.

Rheumatism: A painful disorder of joints or muscles not directly due to infection or injury. This rather ill-defined group includes rheumatic fever (acute rheumatism), rheumatoid arthritis, osteo-arthritis, gout, and "fibrositis"—itself an ill-defined group of disorders in which pain felt in muscles is the common factor.

Rheumatoid-arthritis: A chronic disease of connective tissue, commoner in women than men. The characteristic feature is a small knot or nodule of unflamed fibrous tissue; these tender nodules are often just under the skin. Any organ may on occasion be affected, but most of the symptoms arise from inflammation of the fibrous connective tissue around joints. Any joint may be affected but the knuckle-joints and wrists tend to suffer most.

The course of the disease varies widely. In most cases the inflammation occurs without doing much damage; though further attacks are possible less often a sort of grumpling inflammation persists and the affected joints are stiffened by damage to their linings of smooth cartilage. In severe cases joints may become crippled. This is partly due to direct damage to the joint linings, and partly to the action of muscles around the joint. The muscles over any seat of inflammation tighten as a defensive reaction, and when this happens around damaged joint, the joint may in time be deformed or even dislocated.

In rare cases, rheumatoid arthritis takes the form of a generalized feverish illness like a protracted attack of rheumatic fever.

The cause of rheumatoid arthritis is not known. There is evidence that it may be an instance of auto-immunity i.e., of a sustained allergic reaction to some component of the patient's own tissues. Physical and emotional stresses play some part in setting off attacks, and there may also be hereditory factors. The immediate damage for joints is probably due to the release of destructive enzymes from inflammed cells, and some research is directed at the source of these. Rheumatoid arthritis is not likely to be completely curable until more is known of its causes, but much can be done to alleviate it.

Osteo-arthritis: Degeneration of joints, with some loss of the almost frictionless cartilage linings and formation of rough deposits of bone. Since there is inflammation, "Osteo arthritis" is the better term. It is one of the seemingly inevitable processes of ageing, affecting mainly the joints subject to most wear and tear from weight-bearing—those of the legs and spine. Joints that have been subjected to abnormal stresses by faulty posture, injury or deformity are especially vulnerable and may develop osteo-arthritis before middle age. There are discomfort or pain, and limitation of movement due to this disease.

Gout: A chemical disease with precipitation of uric acid crystal in the tissues. Most of the symptoms are caused by crystals around joints, often single joints.

There are numerous sources of the uric acid in the body. It is a break-down product of nucleic acid, an essential component of all living matter. All foods contain some. The highest concentrations are in animal products such as kidney and liver, and vegetable seeds such as peas (kesari-ki-dal is one of the pea species that causes crippling joint disease). A more important source than the diet is the regular break-down of the body's own cells; and uric acid is also synthesised from ammonia formed in the body. In a healthy person the concentration in the blood and tissue fluids is kept to about 0.02 percent by excreting any excess in the urine. The solubility of uric acid is about 0.06 per cent. Above this level, crystal may be precipitated and gout develops. The excess could arise in three ways; too much in diet, too much synthesised in the body, and too little excreted by the kidneys. Unfortunately diet is usually the least important, otherwise gout could be controlled simply by cutting out unsuitable food. Oversynthesis, due to an inherited biochemical anomaly, is much more significant. Defective exeretion may arise from a similar fault, and also gout is occasionally a complication of kidney disease.

A classic attack of gout begins without warning, often middle of the night. A single joint, proverbially at the base of the big toe, is suddenly inflammed and extremely painful. After a day or two the symptoms vanish, but the attack may be repeated at any time, not necessarily in the same joint. Injury predisposes a joint to gout. A bout of heavy drinking can set off an attack by interfering with the excretion of uric acid, but as often as not there is no evident reason for the attack to start.

After many attacks a joint can become permanently deformed, with large deposits of uric acid in the bones e.g., of the knuckles.

Although the main symptoms, arise from affected joints, the real danger of gout is damage to the kidneys by uric acid crystals, which can ultimately lead to a condition like Bright's disease (disorder of kidney) associated with retention of water in the body and loss of protein in the urine followed by nephritis (inflammed kidneys). Untreated gout is also associated with degeneration of arteries and its complications.

Many plants are available for the management of joint's diseases.

Role of Plants

1. Colchicum luteum, Baker

Family : Liliaceae

Names	:	Hindi	–	Harantutiya
		Sanskrit	–	Hiranyatutha
		English	–	Golden Collyrium
		Punjabi	–	Surinjan-e-talkh
		Urdu	–	Suranjanetalkh

Description: An annual herb; corms brownish in colour, almost conical in shape, with one side flat, the other roundish. Leaves narrow but broader towards the tip, inceasing in size as the plant approaches fruiting stage, 15-30 cm long, 0.8-1.5 cm broad. Flowers large, 2.5-4 cm diameter, 7-10 cm long, yellow. Fruits 2.5-4 cm long, their beaks recurved.

Distribution: Plant is found in Himalayas 700 to, 2, 800 altitude, usually in outskirts of forest or in open grassy places. Available in Market on Ayurvedic or Unani/ Homoeopathic shops.

Parts used: Corms and seeds.

Properties: Alterant, carminative, laxative, aphrodisiac,

Phytochemicals: Alkaloid-colchicine of dried corm and seeds.

Forms of use: Powder (125 to 300 mg) and extract (25 to 30 mg).

Medicinal Uses

The fresh corms of the plant collected before its flowering season constitute the drug *colchicum corm* and the ripe dried seeds, the drug *colchicum* seed.

The corms contain the active principle colchicine, it is useful in pains and inflammation of gout. Clinical experiment with colchicum in small doses over a long period have shown success in about sixty per cent of patients. It is also applied externally in paste to reduce swelling and pain.

Its other uses are in the diseases of liver and spleen.

2. Boswellia serrata, Roxb.

Family : Burseraceae

Names : Hindi – Luban
Sanskrit – Shallaki
English – Indian olibanum
Bengali – Salaidhoopa
Gujarati – Dhupro
Tamil – Parangi saambraani
Trade name – Salaigonda, Salai guggul

Description: Bark thick and aromatic leaves look like neem leaves. Flowers small, its aromatic and white. Fruit contains single compressed seed. When its bark is cut, a secretion exudes which becomes gum-like after exposure to air. The drug consists of oleo-gum resin. The material sometimes occurs as lumps of agglutinated tears.

Distribution: Mountainous tracks of central India. Bihar, Orissa and North Gujarat etc.

Parts used: Bark and gum.

Properties: Refrigerant, diuretic, demulcent, aperient alterant and emmenagogue.

Phytochemicals : Gum, aromatic, oil, resin and phytosterols.

Forms of use: Gum resin and bark decoction.

Medicinal Uses

A paste made of the gum resin with coconut oil or lemon juice is applied over indolent swellings and in rheumatism.

Its other uses are in skin diseases, cystic breast, lung diseases, gonorrhoea, piles etc.

3. Apium graveolens. Linn

Family : Umbelliferae
Names : Hindi – Ajmoda
Sanskrit – Ajmoda
English – Celery
Gujarati – Ajamoda
Bengali – Randhuni
Kannada – Ajamoda voma

Marathi	–	Ajamoda vova
Tamil	–	Asham taagam
Trade name	–	Ajamoda

Description: It is biennial erect herb about 2 to 3 ft high. Leaves pinnate, arising from the roots, the fruit is small about 1mm long and 1mm in diameter and contains minute seeds.

Distribution: Found at the base of the north western Himalayas and outlying hills in the Punjab and in Western India.

Parts used: Root and seeds.

Properties: Tonic, carminative, diuretic, emmenagogue, stimulant and antirheumatic.

Phytochemicals: Glycosides, terpenes, furocoumarins and volatile oil besides minerels and vitamin A and C.

Forms of use: Seed powder.

Medicinal Uses

It has been successfully employed in rheumatoid arthritis.

Its other uses are as diuretic, stomachic, aphrodisiac and tonic. As antispasmodic, it is used in bronchitis and asthma.

Other Useful Plants

- *Glycyrrhiza glabra* **(Mulathee)**—It is powerful anti-inflammatory agent. It used for the treatment of rheumatoid arthritis and various inflammatory conditions.
- *Vanda roxbughil* **(Rasna)**—Its root is used against inflammation, rheumatic pains and tremors.
- *Piper longum* **(Lal-mirch)**—It is very useful in gout, rheumatism and lumbago.
- *Mentha piperita* **(Vilayati Podina)**—Peppermint oil obtained from it is used in medicine for rheumatic and other pains.

- *Gaultheria fragrantissima* **(Gandhpura-ka-tel)**—It is also called oil of winter green, used in treatment of various forms of rheumatism.
- *Ricinus communis* **(Arandi)**—Its half warmed leaves are applied on joints to relieve pain (It is for better results—apply warm mustard oil over the joints and cover it with Arandi leaves, keep doing it for 10-15 days for complete relief).

Medicines

Ayurvedic	:	Vatreene Tablet
	:	Mahanarayan Taila
	:	Prasarini Taila
Unani medicines	:	Majoon Suranjan
	:	Majoon Auja
	:	Majoon Chobchini
Homeopathic	:	Rhustox 30 and Arnica 30 (alternate with 2 hr gap)
	:	Rhustox complex
	:	Ledum complex (Gout)

13 (a)

Plant Drugs Prepared by Allopathic Drug Companies

D = Drug P = Plant C = Company U = Use

1. D – Vincristine
   P – *Catharanthus roseus*
   C – Cipla and Biochem
   U – Cancer

2. D – Etoposide
   P – *Podophyllum peltatum*
   C – Khandelwal
   U – Cancer

3. D – Fatlow
   P – Guggal, Triphalla, Ketuki & Chitrak
   C – Gentech & Hundiya
   U – Anti-obesity

4. D – Heptoguard
   P – *A. paniculata, P. kurroa & P. nuriri*
   C – Thomis Pharma
   U – Liver disorder

5. D – Renergy
   P – ***Genseng, Withania somnifera, Asparagus racemosus***
   C – Lupin
   U – Tonic/nutrition

6. D – Kamillosan
   P – *Matricasia chamonilla*
   C – German Remedies
   U – Skin disease

7. D – Cineraria drops
   P – *Cineraria maritima*

C – Haslab
U – Eyes

8. D – Tusidac
P – *Adhatoda vasica, Albissia lebbeck & Cleodendrum seratum*
C – Alidac
U – Cough & cold

9. D – Ergotab
P – *Ergot alkaloids*
C – Jagsonpal
U – Uterine stimulent

10. D – Laxena
P – Leaves of Sanai
C – Alpine
U – Constipation

11. D – Ecomint
P – *Mentha piperita*
C – Smith Kline
U – Irritable colon

12. D – Bilovas
P – *Ginkoflavone glycosides*
C – German Remedies
U – Cerebral activator

13. D – Nervomine
P – *Passiflora ext.*
Crataegus ext.
C – Franco-Indian
U – Tranquilizer

14. D – Quinidine
P – Alkaloids of Cinchena bark
C – Wellcome
U – Anti-arrhythmic

15. D – Sepasil
P – *Rawolfia serpentina*
C – Novartis
U – Anti hypertensive

16. D – Digoxin
    P – *Digitalis purpurea*
    C – Wellcome
    U – Congestive heart faiture

17. D – Auxicalm
    P – *Nardostachys jatamansi, Withania somnifera, Valeriana wallichi & Acorus calamus*
    C – Lupin
    U – Tranquilizer

18. D – Kalpastic
    P – Plant glycoside-Rutin
    C – B.D.H.
    U – Epistaxis, haemorrhage

19. D – Daflan
    P – Flavonoid plant pdt.
    C – Serdia
    U – Piles

20. D – Morcontin CR
    P – Opium alkaloid
    C – Modi-mundi
    U – Analgesic

21. D – Guglip
    P – Commiphora mukul
    C – Cipla
    U – Cardiotonic

22. D – Sallaki
    P – Bossawclla scrvata
    C – Lupia
    U – Arthritis

13 (b)

Comparative Study of Herbal Preparations of Baidyanath and Hamdard

Sl. No.	Medicine	Uses	Doses	Company
1.	Amoebica Tablet	Amoebic dysentery	1-2 Tablet thrice daily	Baidyanath
2.	Pench, Jwarish Amla	Dysentery & diarrhoea	2 tsp thrice daily	Hamdard
3.	Katujarist	Bacillary dysentery & diarrhoea	–do–	Baidyanath
4.	Vatrina Tablet	Rheumatic complaints	1-2 Tablet thrice daily	Baidyanath
5.	Majoon Suranjan	–do–	5-10 g with water at bedtime	Hamdard
6.	Majoon Aujai	–do–	–do–	–do–

Cont'd...

Sl. No.	Medicine	Uses	Doses	Company
7.	Shankhpushpi Syrup	Improves memory	20-30 ml a day	Baidyanath
8.	Khamira Gavziban Ambari (Jawaharwala)	–do– stomach	5 g with water early morning on empty	Hamdard
9.	Khamira Gauziban Ambari (Sada)	–do–	–do–	–do–
10.	Vita-Ex Tablet	Vigour & strength	1-2 Tablet with milk twice daily	Baidyanath
11.	Rhuma oil	Rheumatic complaints	Apply on the affected part of the body	Baidyanath
12.	Lahmina	Vigour & strength	1 tsp thrice daily	Hamdard
13.	Suparipak	–do–	5-10 g with milk once at bedtime	Baidyanath & Hamdard
14.	Swaskalp Tablet	Asthma & Esniphilia	1-2 tablet thrice daily	Baidyanath

Cont'd...

Sl. No.	Medicine	Uses	Doses	Company
15.	Sharbat zufa Murakkab	–do–	25-50 ml with warm water twice daily	Hamdard
16.	Sharbat Rabvi	–do–	–do–	–do–
17.	Habbe Zikunnafs	–do–	One tablet twice with honey	–do–
18.	Pathrina Tablet	Antacid, used in stone in gall bladder and in urinary trouble	2 tablets thrice daily	Baidyanath
19.	Majoon Hijrulyahud	–do–	5 g with water twice daily	Hamdard
20.	Krimimudgar Ras Tablet	Intestinal worms	1 tablet twice daily with honey	Baidyanath
21.	Kurs Dedan	Intestinal worms	2 tablet with water in the morning	Hamdard

Cont'd...

Sl. No.	Medicine	Uses	Doses	Company
22.	Itriphal Dedan	–do–	10 g with water at bedtime, take 3 days	–do–
23.	Hazamyum	Antacid, in dyspepsia colic gas troubles	2 tsp three times a day with water	Baidyanath
24.	Jawaris Kamuni	In dyspepsia, colic gas trouble	2 tsp three times a day with water	Hamdard
25.	Jawaris Jalinoos	–do–	5 g with water twice in a day	–do–
26.	Kabjahar	Constipation	3-4 g with warm water at bedtime	Baidyanath
27.	Shodhi Harre	Constipation & indigestion	To be sucked	–do–
28.	Hubbe Mukavi Meda	Give strength to stomach and liver	1-2 tablet thrice daily	Hamdard

Cont'd...

Sl. No.	Medicine	Uses	Doses	Company
29.	Sundari Kalp Special	Restores hormonal balance, keeps women healthy	3 tsp thrice daily	Baidyanath
30.	Mustoorin	–do–	3 tsp thrice daily	Hamdard
31.	Joshina	Cold and cough	2 tsp thrice daily	Hamdard
32.	Lauq Sapinsta	Cough	5-10 g twice daily with warm water	–do–
33.	Khamira Ganzaba Ambari/Jawaharwala	Strengthens brain & heart function, controls palpitation	5-10 g once in the morning with water	–do–
34.	Manikya Pishti	Nervine heart tonic	125 mg twice daily with water	Baidyanath
35.	Makaradhwaj Sadgun Valijant	–do–	30-50 mg daily with milk or water	–do–

Cont'd...

Sl. No.	Medicine	Uses	Doses	Company
36.	Rhuma oil	Rheumatic disorders, spondylosis Lumbago a day	Apply on the affected part twice/thrice	–do–
37.	Shankha Pushpi Syrup	Improves memory	20-30 ml twice in a day	–do–
38.	Pirrhoid tab	Useful in piles	1-2 tab twice a day	–do–
39.	Vita-Ex-Gold (Cap)	For stamina and vitality	1-2 capsule twice a day	Baidyanath
40.	Roghan Badam Shirin.	For perfect health and glow	1-2 tsp once a day with milk	Hamdard
41.	Chaivanprash	A reputed Ayurvedic medicine for general well being and cough/cold	1 tsp thrice a day with water	Baidyanath

Cont'd...

Sl. No.	Medicine	Uses	Doses	Company
42.	Hamdogen	When you want to feel young	1 cap. daily with milk	Hamdard
43.	Sualin	For quick relief from all kinds of cough water	1 tablet thrice a day with tea or warm water	–do–
44.	Sadoori	The most effective cough syrup	1 tsp thrice a day.	–do–
45.	Safi	The natural blood purifier	1 tsp thrice a day	–do–
46.	Sinkara	Family tonic, improves the mental power	1 tsp thrice a day with water	Hamdard
47.	Naunihal Gripe Syrup	For common ailment in children (constipation, indigestion, diarrhoea)	1 tsp thrice a day with water	Hamdard

Cont'd...

Sl. No.	Medicine	Uses	Doses	Company
48.	Majoon kundur	Useful for kidney and urinary bladder	5-10 g twice daily with water	–do–
49.	Basant Kusumakar Ras	Tonic for heart and brain, urinary infection, asthma and general weakness	One pill in a day with honey	Baidyanath
50.	Chitrak Haritaki	Useful in chronic cough, bronchitis and corzya	1-2 g with milk twice daily	–do–

13 (c)
Herbal Tips

1. Constipation

a. The best way to deal with constipation is to change food habits. Milk boiled vegetables, fruits and their juices should be taken in large quantities, together with foods containing a lot of roughage & fibrous matter.

b. 10 g of Senna leaves and 5 g of aniseed should be boiled in a cup of water with sugar, then strained and drunk before retiring for the night.

c. Half a litre of milk mixed with 50 g of khand taken at night will give relief.

d. Another remedy is to eat 40 g of Gulkand with milk everyday.

e. If these remedies fail to give relief, 6 g of the rind of harr should be finely powdered and mixed with a little luke warm water and salt be taken.

f. Take *Bathua ka saag* during the season for getting rid of obstinate constipation.

2. Toothache

a. A paste made of finely ground leaves of tulsi should be warmed a little and applied to the aching tooth.

b. Ginger ground into a paste with a pinch of salt also relieves toothache.

c. Applying clove oil is also effective.

d. Brush your teeth with dried, powdered leaves of tulsi to strengthen gums and prevent pain & pyorrhoea.

e. Brush your teeth after each meal to keep away dental

problems.

f. Avoid chewing tobacco, pan-masala and other similar items to avoid early decay.

g. Wash and dry neem leaves; grind them to a fine powder. Sprinkle this powder over the toothpaste before brushing your teeth. You will never have complaints of tooth decay or any mouth diseases.

3. **(A) For Vigour**

Onion juice	...	2 tsp
Honey	...	2 tsp
Adrak juice	...	1 tsp

To be taken twice, morning and evening for ten or fifteen days.

(B) For Vigour and Strength

Onion juice	...	2 tsp
Honey	...	2 tsp
Desi-ghee	...	2 tsp
Egg yolk	...	1 egg

Mix the above materials and warm it on stove, add Misri and take once in the morning for 15 days.

4. **Leucoderma or White Spot on Skin**

(If it is senseless, it could be leprosy then do not use this prescription)

Eat *Bathua ka saag* daily during the season in form of Roti or Daal-sag and use its juice over spots daily at least 2/3 times. Eat Anjir regularly for a month.

5. **For Malaria**

Tulsi	...	10 leaves
Bhang	...	5 leaves
Kali-mirch	...	10-15 pieces

Grind the above mixture to a paste and make pea size pellets. Dry it in shade. Two pellets three times a day.

6. **For Nausea**

(a) Neebu-pani at the time of nausea will be helpful.

(b) Soft kheera should be eaten gradually to get rid of obstinate nauseatic condition.

7. For Purifying Blood

A plant commonly called Mundi, its aqueous extract (one cup) daily purifies the blood.

8. For Angina and Ischaemic Heart Disease

1. Puskarmula
2. Arjun
3. Kut
4. Prishnaparini
5. Guggulu

Above plants are equally powdered and 10g powder is left overnight in a cup of water and taken in the morning.

9. Fever/Headache/Bodyache/Malaria

1. Ghiraita	...	5 leaves
2. Neem leaves	...	5 leaves
3. Tulsi	...	10 leaves
4. Lemon Grass	...	5 leaves
5. Black pepper	...	10-15 pieces

Mix all, boil & strain, add sugar to taste. Take half cup 3 times a day.

10. Dysentery/Tenusmus/Diarrhoea

(a) Grind whole plant of Duddhi in water. Strained water extract (half cup) if taken 2/3 times a day gives quick relief.

(b) Grind a lemon (including the seeds and the rind) to a paste, with a little salt. It makes an effective cure for diarrhoea.

(c) Hari Harr & choti Harr half roasted in oven and powdered. This powder, mixed with a pinch of black salt, if taken three times (1/2 tsp) will bring prompt relief.

11. For Cold

Tulsi	...	10 leaves

Honey ... 2 tsp

Make paste of leaves and mix with honey. Taken in the morning, it will keep out cold & cough away and will also help in bringing down blood pressure.

12. Eczema

(a) Apply garlic juice & lemon juice to the affected place. It will clear fungus infection.

(b) Eczema/fungus infection of nails, hand & feet will be cleared with the use of Mehndi (Use continuously for a week). Avoid excess indulgence in water.

(c) Use of tulsi leaves and lemon juice to the infected part will also cure eczema.

13. High Blood Pressure

(a) 1. Garlic ... 5 cloves
2. Tulsi ... 5 leaves
3. Honey ... 4 tsp

Make a paste of above ingredients and eat it once in the morning without taking anything.

(b) Eat two bananas daily to balance excess sodium in the body. Banana contains enough potassium to cut all effects of sodium (we use as common salt).

14. Stomach Upsets

1. Tulsi ... 5 leaves
2. Adrak ... Few pieces
3. Black Pepper ... 10-15 pieces

Boil these material. Strain and drink 2/3 times (half cup).

15. Cough

(a) Dip pieces of one medium size onion in 10 ml of pure honey, leave it overnight. Remove the pieces and take one teaspoonful juice 3 times a day.

— Muli as vegetable
— Anar & Angur juice
— Liv-52 Tablet, 2 tablet 3 times a day
— Take rest.

21. Cuts/Wounds

(a) Sprinkle powdered Mehndi or

(b) Sprinkle powdered Haldi.

22. Arthritis/Gout

(a) Boil mustard oil (10ml) with one moderate pack of Garlic bulb, apply on the affected parts 3/4 times a day.

(b) Massage with camphor oil 3/4 times a day on the affected parts.

(c) Apply warm mustard oil on the affected parts at the time of bed rest and cover them with Dhatura leaves overnight. Keep doing it for 15 days. Repeat again as per need.

(d) Massage with Turpentine oil/Eucalyptus oil 3/4 times a day on the affected part. Cover that portion with a wet towel and gradually pour hot water (not very hot) from kettle on it. Great relief.

23. For Body Resistance to Disease

A mixture of amla, harr, bahera and herb giloya (1:1:1:1) if taken regularly makes the person immune to illness.

24. To Stop Oozing Blood

Sprinkle haldi powder, flowing of blood will be stopped.

25. Hoarse Voice

Sprinkle common salt on the small pieces of adrak. Take the pieces gradually one by one.

26. Eyebrow

Put a little warm castor oil on scanty eyebrows. This will enhance their growth.

27. Hair

(a) Extract the juice of the aloe-vera plant and rub it into your scalp. This ensures the healthy growth of hair.

(b) For glowing hair, grind a few whole green grams,

lemon peels, a handful of curry leaves and a few "rithas" to a paste and apply to the hair before washing off.

28. Insect Bite

To cure an insect bite apply any balm on it. It will relieve you of the itchy sensation

29. Kidneys

Dry tulsi seeds and grind them with an equal quantity of sugar. One teaspoonful of this powder, taken every morning, is good for the kidney.

30. Sore Throat

Drink tea with a pinch of pepper to get relief from bad throat.

31. Skin

Banana is a natural skin whitener. Mash a ripe banana and apply it on the face and neck, and your tan colour will fade away.

32. Hiccups

Roast some peppercorns and breathe deeply. Your hiccups will stop at once.

33. Dysentery

A teaspoonful of fenugreek seeds in a glass of lukewarm water will bring relief immediately.

34. Liver

To maintain your liver in a good condition, eat a refrigerated pineapple slice dipped in honey, twice a day.

35. Hair

A mixture of almond oil, olive oil and castor oil in equal proportions acts as an excellent hair tonic.

36. Insects

(a) Place neem leaves in your books to prevent them from being attacked by insects.

(b) Burn neem leaves in the courtyard or garden to keep mosquitoes away.

37. Cold

Drink plenty of lime juice everyday as the ascorbic acid (Vitamin C) content of lime helps heal wounds quickly, maintain your teeth, helps also hair, nails and complexion in good condition and guard against catching colds.

38. Nose

Stop nose-bleeds by putting a few drops of pomegranate juice into your nostrils.

39. Lips

Massage your lips with coriander leaf juice for soft and rosy results.

40. Eyes

(a) Place cotton wool swabs dipped in cold milk on closed eyes to soothe the eyes and remove dark circles.

(b) Triphalla (Amla+Harr+Bahera) soaked in water overnight then boiled & filtered. The filtrate to be applied to the eyes along with rose water.

41. Cough

If your suffering from a nagging cough or chest congestion, boil three cups water with two fresh betal leaves & four crushed peppercorns, till the water is reduced to half. Strain and drink it every morning and night with a teaspoonful of honey added to it.

42. Medicinal Value of Basil Leaves

(a) For immediate relief from toothache, take two basil leaves, a grain of salt and a pinch of pepper powder and press against the affected tooth.

(b) Mix equal quantities of basil juice, honey, and caraway seed (Ajwain) juice and drink on an empty stomach if you are suffering from cough.

43. Tea

Tea is a wonderful drink. Brew your tea slowly, it takes three-four minutes for the anti-oxidants to make their way into the water. Anti-oxidants delay ageing.

44. Motion Sickness

Chewing a couple of cloves while travelling will relieve motion sickness.

45. High B.P.

If you are suffering from high blood pressure, try this remedy. Boil two cups water with 10 to 15 basil leaves, a few peppercorns and a little sugar. Strain and drink it thrice a day.

46. Toothache

Take one teaspoonful ginger juice, a little edible camphor, a little honey and a pinch of salt. Heat the mixture for a second and apply it on the aching tooth. You will get immediate relief.

47. Sore Throat

Powder peppercorns and basil leaves and dry them in the shade. Use this powder to make black tea.

48. Hair Loss

Don't throw away lemon rinds, orange peels and pomegranate skin. Just dry them in the sun and grind to a fine powder. Mix this powder in coconut oil and apply to your hair to prevent hair loss and for glossy hair.

49. Acidity and Indigestion

Dry roast one teaspoonful each of cumin seeds and caraway seeds (ajwain) in a pan. Add one cup water and boil till it is reduced to half its quantity. Strain and add sugar to taste. Drink one teaspoonful for relief from acidity and indigestion.

50. Nausea & Stomach Ailments

Eat a slice of fresh ginger after each meal to protect yourself, from stomach ailments. For immediate relief from nausea, chew salted dry ginger sticks.

51. Stomach Upsets

For quick relief from an upset stomach, chew a teaspoonful of 'ajwain' (fennel seeds) with little black salt.

52. Cough, Nausea and Vomiting

Take half a cup of onion juice mixed with two teaspoonfuls of honey for relief from cough, nausea & vomiting.

53. Toxicity

To check if mushrooms are poisonous, boil them in water along with a few garlic flakes. If water turns black they are poisonous.

54. Enuresis (Passing Urine at Night)

Chewing one teaspoonful of black sesame seeds (til) before going to bed is a sure shot treatment for such problem.

55. Malnutrition

Banana is a complete food. It has all the ingredients necessary for body's nutrition, growth & strength. So, it is specially recommended for children and old people. But it causes a little bit constipation so, it should be taken with black pepper & salt.

56. Habitual Abortion

Grind fresh flowers of Anar (2g) to a fine paste. Add a little water and filter. Add sugar to taste in filtrate and use it morning and evening (taking 2g flower each time) for three days.

57. Nausea/Bile

Sharbat of Imli cools liver/bile and checks nausea and vomiting especially in summer days. Dip 5g ripe fruit of Imli in water for 1/2 hours, after that it is masticated in water and seeds are thrown out. Now, remaining water containing imli is taken in the afternoon with sugar.

58. Dropsy/Liver Inflammation

Leaves of Kasondi (1g) and Kali mirch (7) are ground

together in water and filtered. Filtrate is to be taken morning and evening for one week (each time 1g kasondi & 7 kali mirch).

59. For all kinds of Fever

Gilo (Gurach)-one gram is powdered and dipped in water. Water is strained and divided in two doses. Mix each dose with a teaspoonful of sugar and take morning and evening. Better if Ajwain (250mg.) is also added to Gilo.

60. Face Cream

Chana ka atta (besan)	...	1/2 Cup
Haldi Powder	...	1 tsp
Mustard Oil	...	1/4 to 1/2 Cup

Mix all these materials to a semi-solid paste and apply it on your face. It will bring marvellous glow on your skin. It can be used on hands & legs also.

61. Cataract

Tobacco leaves	...	1 grams
Arandi ka Tel	...	4 grams

Mix these material to very fine paste and keep it in a small bottle. Apply it to eyes with a rod daily.

62. Cough

White Pepper	...	1 gram
Misri	...	250 mg

Grind these items to a very fine powder. Now mix it with one tsp Malai and take it bit by bit rather lick it gradually.

63. Fever

Mix equal number of leaves of Tulsi, Neem and Lemon grass plus 7-10 black pepper. Boil it like making tea. Strain the water and drink 3/4 times a day.

64. Gas/Giddiness

Dhania powder	...	1 gram
Khand	...	250 mg

Mix these two materials in the said ratio and keep it in

a container, use two tsp after each meal with water.

65. Piles

While going to toilet, put a medium piece of Alum (Fitkari) in water. Use this water after the toilet. Repeat till relief.

66. DIARRHOEA/INDIGESTION/GAS

Saunf and Dhania is to be mixed in equal proportion, powdered and a small amount of Misri or Khand is added. 2 tsp is to be taken morning and evening. This will stop diarrhoea/indigestion/gas formation and is helpful to eyes.

67. Eye Sight

One small piece of haldi is kept in lemon and when it dries, haldi is taken out & put in second fresh lemon and when it dries it is further kept in third/fourth lemon. Now, Haldi is ground with one/two drops of water & applied on the eyes with the help of a rod for 7/10 days or as needed.

68. Cholera

Mix powdered red pepper with honey and prepare fine small pellets (equal to 1/2 pea size). Use 2 pellets when patient feels extreme weakness. It will bring dramatic relief in 2/3 days.

69. Dog-bite

In case of dog-bite, first apply mustard oil on that part and then pack it with red pepper powder. It will check disease from spreading even if the dog is rabid.

70. Leprosy

Red Pepper (Powdered)	...	1 g
Ghee	...	2.5 g

Mix and keep it in a small container. Use it on the affected part 2/3 times a day. It will bring good results.

71. Abortion

Tender leaves of Babool	...	2 g

Water ... 2 Cups

Boil it so that water becomes one cup. Strain, add Misri to taste. Use this 2/3 days once a day to check abortion.

72. Dandruff

Add a few drops of eucalyptus oil to the henna mixture before applying it on your hair if you want, dark copper colour. This also helps to get rid of dandruff and leaves your hair shining.

73. Toothache

For instant relief from severe toothache, press a little turmeric powder into the tooth.

74. High Blood Pressure

To control high blood pressure, mix equal quantities of onion juice and honey and take one teaspoonful every day in the morning.

75. Diarrhoea

(a) A strong cup of unsweetened black tea is effective in stopping diarrhoea.

(b) Another quick remedy is to peel apple and shred it. Keep the shredded pieces in a plate for approx. 20 minutes until they turn brown in colour, and then eat them.

76. Constipation

Simply eat a few liquorice sticks. One of its many properties is that it is a natural laxative.

77. Catarrh

To rid yourself of congestion, mix a teaspoonful of vinegar in a glass of warm water and sip frequently.

78. Coughs

First cut an onion or several flakes of garlic into thin slices. Cover the slices with honey and leaves for two to three hours. Drink a spoonful of the resulting juice throughout the day.

79. Smelly Feet

Soak your feet in strong tea for 20 minutes every day until smell disappears. To prepare your footbath, brew two tea bags in 500 ml of water for 15 minutes and pour the tea into a basin containing two litres of cool water.

80. Bleeding Gums

Take lemon juice in a glass of water daily for 3/4 days. Also gargle with salt.

81. Chills

Instead of your regular hot tea or coffee, have a glass of hot water mixed with honey and lemon. Put a teaspoonful of honey, lemon juice and a little grated ginger in a glass and add hot water, stir & drink.

82. Cracked SKin

Apply a mixture of grated potato soaked in olive oil. Leave this for 10 minutes and then rinse off.

83. Tired Eyes

Lavender oil offers gentle relief for tired and strained eyes. Add a drop of lavender oil to 500 ml of water & shake the solution well. Dip two cotton wool pads in the liquid, squeeze out the excess water and place one pad over each eyes (Don't use contact lenses at this time)

84. For General Debility

Sage is an excellent pick-me-up. Take 100 g of fresh sage leaves and soak them in a bottle of white wine for two weeks. Add honey for sweetening and leave for an extra 24 hours. Use a muslin cloth for straining, making sure you press as you strain. Collect the solution in a bottle and drink a little before meals.

85. Spots

Herbs like tea tree oil and lavender oil, both antiseptics, can be applied neatly and quickly to pimples.

86. Warts

Place some chopped onions in a dish, cover with salt and leave overnight. Twice a day apply the resulting juice to the warts until they disappear.

87. Bad Breath

Parsley leaves are rich in chlorophyll, nature's own deodoriser. Chew some leaves regularly and your breath will remain fresh. Alternatively, you can chew some cardamom seeds to sweeten your breath.

88. Indigestion

Place a teaspoonful of freshly grated ginger into a pan and add a cup of water. Cover and allow to simmer for five minutes. Strain the contents & drink.

89. Nausea

Powdered cinnamon and sliced ginger work by interrupting nausea signals sent from the stomach to the brain. If you are a herbal tea drinker, simply sprinkle powdered cinnamon on the tea and drink. drink ginger-tea to check nausea.

90. Nose Bleeds

Dip a cotton bud in rose water and dab it on to the inside of your nostrils to stop the bleeding.

91. Bruises

Slice a raw onion and place over the bruise. But do not apply this over grave injuries.

92. Toothache

Cloves are excellent painkillers. You can either chew one, or place it near the tooth. As the juices flow and mix with saliva, they numb the gum and alleviate pain.

93. Stomach Belches

Eat a small piece of jaggery after eating radish, you can avoid unpleasant belches.

94. Constipation

If you are often constipated, eat more lady finger 'Sabji'.

95. Haemoglobin

Prepare leafy vegetable 'Sabji' in an iron 'Kadai'. It will taste good. The 'Kadai' is a good source of iron which is required to increase haemoglobin in blood.

96. Malaria

Eating a leaf or two of tulsi takes care of many disorders and works wonders during malaria.

97. Sprain

Add a tsp of salt to two tsp turmeric powder and boil with a little water to obtain a thick paste. Apply while still hot over sprain.

98. Thirst

Eat a cardamom or two, especially during long journeys, to avoid feeling thirsty.

99. Nails

For glossy and strong nails, soak them in a mixture of lemon juice & glycerine.

100. To Check Bleeding

Sprinkle powdered haldi and henna over the oozing blood. This will stop flow of blood immediately.

14

Miracles of Water Therapy

A recent report by the Washington-based Worldwatch Institute has concluded that one of the first and foremost basic changes that lengthens life expectancy is the supply of clean water. It adds that this perhaps is the reason why the average Indian's life expectancy has increased by about 20 years during the last 45 years. For the people of Kerala too, availability of safe drinking water has been responsible for much higher life expectancy—73 years, for men and 68 years for women.

Water is the elixir of life and the second most vital need for the survival of mankind–after air. It is commonly understood that safe drinking water can be the vital link between life & death.

It might sound incredible, but facts cannot be denied too. As said by Confucius nearly 2500 years back, the health of an organism is tempered wholly by the mechanics of the stomach. As a modern saint, Paramahansa Yogananda analysed, it is overeating (or eating on all the 365 days of a year) that leads to and complicates diseases.

Before discussing the details, one might be interested to know some of the diseases which can be cured under this therapy.

Headache, hypertension, anaemia, rheumatism, general paralysis, obesity, arthritis, sinusitis, tachycardia, anaesthesia.

Cough, asthama, bronchitis, pulmenary tuberculosis, menigitis, hepatic diseases, urogenital diseases. Hyperacidity, gastritis, dysentery, rectal prolapses, constipation, haemorrhoids, diabetes.

Eye troubles, opthalmic haemorrhage, opthalmia, irregular menstruation, Leucorrhoea, uterine cancer, cancer of the mammary glands, Rhinitis Laryngitis.

About heart disease it is mentioned that "who drank atleast 5 glasses of water per day had a 50% lower risk of fatal heart attack than who drank 2 glasses or less. However, one should drink 8 glasses of water per day".

How can one practise water therapy? Every morning as soon as one gets up, what one has to do is not wash one's mouth and face but drink 1.26 kg (1260 cc) of water at a stretch, only then should one wash one's face.

For the next 45 minutes one should not eat nor take beverages.

All this should be preceded by some preparations. After the last night's dinner (before going to bed) one should not eat nor drink stimulating beverages or soft drinks.

While following this therapy, one should drink water two hours after a meal. One should not consume any drinks containing snacks/fast food before going to bed.

Where water contains impurities, it should be boiled in the night to be used in the morning.

Experience has shown that following diseases were cured by water therapy within the time shown below:–

Hypertension	...	One month
Gastricpatosis	...	Two days
Constipation	...	One day
Diabetes	...	One week
Cancer	...	One month
Pulmonary tuberculosis	...	Three months

Person suffering from arthritis and rheumatism should use water therapy three times a day for one week and thereafter once in a day.

If you have the nagging problem of bad breath, drink at least five glasses of water first thing in the morning. This is an instant remedy for bad breath, besides keeping your system clean.

15

Some Herbal Preparations of Himalayan Drug Company

As it is quite evident that plants are the prolific sources of medicines since time immemorial and herbal preparations at one time were the only remedy for all kinds of diseases. The Himalayan Drug Company is an effort in this direction and is doing good job. Some of its preparations are mentioned here as follows:

(from next page)

Sl. No.	Name of Drug	Main plants used	Doses	Usefulness
1.	Abana tablet	Terminallia arjuna (Arjun) Withania somnifera (Ashwagandha) Emblica officinalis (Vidanga) Asparagus racemosus (Shatavari) Napeta hindustana (Billilotan) Eclipta alba (Bhringraj) Boerhavia diffusa (Punarva)	2 x BD	A cardiac tonic that protects the heart, guards against circulatory problems and wards off the fears and anxieties which often lead to cardiac neurosis.
2.	Bonnisan syrup	Tinospora corditolia (Guduchi) Piper longum (Pipali) Cichorium intybus (Kasni) Terminalia chebula (Har) Tribulus terrestris (Gokhru)	Two spoonful, 3 times	Keeps babies healthy, playful and happy, clears griping stomach pain, good for common digestive disorders.
3.	Cystone tablet	Vernonia cinerea (Shilapuspa) Rubia cordifolia (Manjishta) Achyranthus aspera (Apamarga) Cyperus scariosus (Nagarmotha)	2 x TDS	Treats urinary tract infections, breaks and expels urinary stones, prevents recurrence.

Cont'd...

Sl. No.	Name of Drug	Main plants used	Doses	Usefulness
4.	Diarex tablet	Holarrhena antidysentrica (Kataja) Symplocos racemosa (Lodhra) Helicteres isora (Murva)	2 x TDS	Stops diarrhoea, treats chronic amoebiasis.
5.	Gasex tablet	Aconitum palmatum (Prativisha) Piper nigrum (Mirch) Embelia ribes (Amailaka)	2 x TDS	Expels gas, relieves gastric uneasiness.
6.	Herbolax tablet	Terminalia chebula (Har) Cichorium intybus (Kasni) Solanum nigrum (Kali-mirch)	2 x OD	Corrects constipation gradually.
7.	Koflet syrup	Adhatoda vasica (Rusa) Vitis vinifera (Draksha) Zingiber officinale (Sonth) Malva sylvestris (Gulkhair) Piper longam (Pipali)	Two spoonful, 3 times	Stops cough fast.

Cont'd...

Sl. No.	Name of Drug	Main plants used	Doses	Usefulness
8.	Liv 52 tablet	Capparis spinosa (Hinsar) Phyllanthus nuriri (Bhumilayaka) Fumaria officinalis (Pitpapra) Andrographis paniculata (Kalmegh)	2 x TDS	For all round care of liver disorder.
9.	Septilin tablet	Guggulu Rubia cordifolia (Manjishta) Glycyrrhiza glabra (Mulethi) Tinsopora cordifolia (Guduchi) Emblica officinalis (Amalaiki)	2 x TDS	Builds up the body's own defence mechanism clears chronic recurrent infections safely.
10.	Lukol tablet	Woodfordia fructosa (Dhataki) Asparagus racemosus (Shatavari) Rawalfia serpentina (Sarpgandha) Boerhaira diffusa (Punarva) Adhatoda vasica (Rusa)	2 x TDS	Controls leucorrhea, checks uterine bleeding, improves blood circulation.

Cont'd...

Sl. No.	Name of Drug	Main plants used	Doses	Usefulness
11.	Mentat tablet	Bacopa monnieri (Brahmi) Withania somnifera (Ashwagandha) Acorus calamus (Vacha) Evolulus alsenoides (Vishnukrantha) Embelica ribes (Amalaiki) Prunus amygdalus (Badam)	2 x BD	Improves memory disturbances, good for stress, anxiety, depression, corrects behavioural disorder.
12.	Pilex tablet	Mimosa pudica (Lajalu) Eclipta alba (Bhringraj) Vitex negundo (Nirgundi) Solanum nigrum (Mirch) Cassia fistula (Aragvadha)	2 x TDS	Relieves painful inflamed bleeding piles, averts surgery. Helps shrink pile masses.
13.	Rumalaya tablet	Rubia cordifolia (Manjishta) Tribulus terrestris (Gokhru) Tinospora cordifolia (Gudachi) Hibiscus abelmoschus (Lata kasturi) Guggul	2 x TDS	Strikes at the root of rheumatic disorders and restores freedom of movement.

Cont'd...

Sl. No.	Name of Drug	Main plants used	Doses	Usefulness
14.	Speman tablet	Orchis mascula (Salabmisri) Astercantha longifolia (Kokilaksha) Lactuca scariola (Kahu) Mucuma prureins (Kapikachu) Laptadenia reticulata (Javanti) Tribulus terrestris (Gokhru)	2 x BD	Often averts surgery in prostatic enlargement, gives hope to childless couple.
15.	Tentex forte tablet	Withania somnifera (Ashwagandha) Crocus sativus (Kumkuma) Tribulus terrestris (Gokhru) Piper longum (Mirch) Mucuna prureins (Kapikachu)	2 x BDS	Non-hormonal safe sex stirmulant for men.

Glossary

Abortifacient: An agent that promotes abortion.

Acne: A pimple-like eruption of the sebaceous glands of the skin, with accumulation of yellow secretion and black overgrowth of the horny layer of the skin.

After-pains: Painful contraction of the womb after child-birth.

Alopecia: A disease of the scalp resulting in complete or partial baldness.

Alternative: A drug which corrects disordered processes of nutrition and restores the normal function of an organ or of the system.

Amenorrhoea: Abnormal suppression of menses.

Anaemia: A deficiency of blood or of red blood-cells or of the red-colouring matter of the blood.

Anasarca: Dropsy.

Angina pectoris: A disease of the heart marked by severe constricting pains in the chest.

Anodyne: A drug that relieves pain.

Antacid: A drug which neutralises the acidity of the gastric juice.

Anthelmintic: A drug that kills intestinal worms.

Antihydrotic: A drug that cures periodic attacks.

Antiphlogistic: A drug which counteracts inflammation.

Antipyretic: A drug which reduces fever.

Antiscorbutic: A drug which prevents or cures scurvy.

Antispasmodic: A drug which counteracts spasmodic disorders.

Aperient: A mild purgative.

Aphrodisiac: A drug which promotes sexual desire.

Aphthae: Minute white ulcers on the tongue and in the mouth.

Apoplexy: Sudden loss of consciousness with some paralysis; stroke.

Ardor urine: A burning sensation while urinating.

Aromatic: A drug which is fragrant, spicy and mildly stimulant.

Ascaris: Intestinal parasitic roundworms.

Ascites: Abdominal dropsy.

Asthma: A chronic disorder of the bronchial tubes.

Astringent: A drug which arrests secretion or bleeding.

Atony: Lack of tension or muscular power.

Attenuent: An agent that dilutes fluids.

Bechic: A remedy for cough.

Bedsores: Ulceration on any part of the body exposed to pressure of bed-ridden patient.

Beriberi: A deficiency disease caused by lack of vitamin B_1.

Blenorrhoea: Excessive mucous discharge, particularly from the uro-genital organs.

Bright's disease: An acute or chronic disease of the kidneys.

Bronchitis: An inflammation of the air passages.

Bronchorrhoea: Excessive discharge from the bronchial mucous membrane.

Calculus: A hard and solid concretion formed in the body, especially in the urinary organs; it may be sand, gravel or stone, according to size.

Cancer: Any malignant growth.

Carbuncle: An acute suppurative inflammation of the skin and tissues under the skin, rapidly spreading around the original point of infection.

Caries: Decay of teeth.

Carminative: A drug which relieves flatulence.

Cathartic: A drug which induces active movement of the bowels.

Caustic: An agent that corrodes or destroys tissues.

Cellulitis: Inflammation of the cellular tissues under the skin.

Chancre: A syphilitic ulcer.

Chilblains: Congestion of the blood at the extremeties as a result of defective blood circulation caused by damp cold.

Cholagogue: A drug which promotes flow of bile.

Chorea: A disease, chiefly in children, marked by irregular, spasmodic and involuntary actions of the limbs and face; St. Vitus's dance.

Chylous urine: Urine with a white milky fluid in which fat globules are in suspension.

Colic: Pain due to spasmodic contraction of the abdomen.

Congestion: An abnormal collection of blood in the blood vessels of any organ or part of the body.

Conjunctivitis: Inflammation of the conjunctiva, the mucous membrane covering the eyeball and lining the eyelids.

Contusion: An injury to the soft parts without breaking the skin.

Counterirritant: An agent which induces a mild irritation or inflammation of the skin to relieve congestion of the deeper structures.

Croup: A diseased condition of the larynx of children characterized by difficult and noisy breathing accompanied by a hoarse cough.

Cystitis: Inflammation of the bladder.

Dandruff: An inflamed condition of the scalp characterized by the presence of white scales in the hair due to the exfoliation of the horny cells of the scalp.

Delirium: An extreme mental disturbance marked by excitement, restlessness and rapid succession of confused and unconnected ideas.

Demulcent: An agent having a soothing effect on the skin and mucous membranes.

Deobstruent: A drug that removes an obstruction to secretion or excretion by opening the natural passages or pores of the body.

Depilatory: An agent that removes or destroys hair.

Diabetes: A wasting disease of metabolism; in one form of the disease, abundant sugar is present continuously in the urine; in the other form, abundant sugar is not present but there is excessive discharge of urine which is of low specific gravity and pale in colour.

Diaphoretic: A drug that induces copious perspiration.

Diphtheria: An infectious disease of the throat and the air passage which become inflamed and swollen and are coated with a fibrinous exudate.

Discutient: A drug which disperses or absorbs a tumour or any coagulated fluid in the body.

Diuretic: A drug which increases the secretion and discharge of urine.

Dropsy: A disease marked by an excessive collection of a watery fluid in the tissues or cavities of the body.

Dysentery: An infectious disease, the chief symptoms of which are acute diarrhoea and discharge of mucus and blood.

Dysmenorrhoea: Unusually painful and difficult menstruation.

Dyspepsia: Indigestion.

Dysuria: Painful and difficult urination.

Eczema: A skin disease accompanied by swelling, redness and exudation of lymph.

Elephantiasis: A disease of the skin caused by a tiny worm and attended with hypertrophy of the affected parts.

Emetic: A drug which induces vomiting.

Emmenagogue: A drug which promotes menstruation or regulates the menstrual periods.

Emollient: A drug which allays irritation of the skin and alleviates swelling and pain.

Enteritis: Inflammation of the intestines.

Epilepsy: A chronic nervous disorder marked by attacks of unconsciousness or convulsions.

Escharotic: An agent capable of destroying tissues.

Excoriation: Removal of the skin by rubbing or chafling.

Expectorant: A drug that promotes the removal of catarrhal matter and phlegm from the bronchial tubes.

Febrifuge: An agent used for reducing fever.

Fistula: An abnormal channel which connects one cavity of the body with another, or which opens out from a cavity to the surface of the body.

Flatulence: A disorder in which there is an excessive collection of gas in the stomach.

Freckles: Coloured spots on the exposed parts of the skin.

Galactagogue: An agent that promotes secretion and flow of milk.

Gleet: A chronic discharge from the urethra.

Glycosuria: A diseased condition of the urine in which sugar is excreted.

Goitre: A chronic enlargement of the thyroid gland.

Gonorrhoea: An infectious venereal disease marked by an inflammatory discharge from the genital organs.

Gravel: A collection of tiny stone-like particles of uric acid, calcium oxalate or phosphates in the organs of the urinary system.

Griping: Sharp pain due to the presence of some irritating substance in the bowels.

Guinea-worm: A very slender worm infecting human beings through drinking contaminated water; it gradually works its way into subcutaneous tissues.

Haemoptysis: Spitting of blood from the lungs or bronchial tubes.

Haemorrhage: Bleeding, especially profuse, from any part of the body.

Heartburn: A burning feeling in the regions of the chest and stomach, generally due to indigestion.

Hemicrania: Migraine.

Hemiplegia: Paralysis of one side of the body.

Hepatic: Pertaining to the liver.

Hepatitis: Inflammation of the liver.

Hernia: Rupture; protrusion through its covering of any organ of the body.

Herpes: A deep-seated vesicular eruption causing neuralgic pains.

Hysteria: A disease in which a physically healthy patient has lost control over acts and feelings and suffers from imaginary ailments.

Indolent: Painless; inactive.

Induration: Area of hardened tissue.

Intermittent fever: Fever which is marked by intervals of normal temperature between periods of rise of temperature.

Itch: An infectious skin disease, caused by a mite, without specific lesions and marked by excessive itching; scabies.

Jaundice: A diseased condition in which there is a yellowish staining of the tissues and excretions with bile.

Lactagogue: Galactagogue.

Lactifuge: A drug that checks the secretion of milk.

Laryngitis: Inflammation of the larynx.

Leprosy: A chronic wasting disease caused by a germ; the disease generally results in mutilations and deformities.

Leucoderma: A condition of the skin in which there is loss of pigment wholly or partially.

Lithontriptic: A drug used for removing calculi or stones formed in the urinary system.

Lochia: The vaginal discharge following childbirth.

Lochiorrhoea: An excessive flow of lochia.

Malaria: A recurrent disease marked by bouts of shivering, sudden rise of temperature and general aching of the body; ague.

Mania: A mental disorder marked by dangerous excitement or insane or morbid craving.

Measles: An infectious febrile disease, chiefly of children, marked by a cold in the head, running of the eyes and nose and appearance of white tiny spots on the inner side of the cheek and of rashes all over the body.

Melancholia: A disorder of the mind marked by depression of spirits and mental sluggishness.

Menopause: Change of life.

Menorrhagia: Abnormally excessive menstruation.

Metrorrhagia: Bleeding from the womb.

Micturation: Urination.

Migraine: Periodic attack of headache affecting one side of the head.

Mumps: An infectious disease marked by the inflammation of the glands near the ear.

Narcotic: A drug which induces deep sleep.

Nausea: A feeling that vomiting is about to take place.

Nephritis: Inflammation of the kidneys.

Neuralgia: Pain felt along a nerve.

Night-blindness: A disease in which the patient is incapable of seeing in the dark.

Ophthalmia: Conjunctivitis.

Orchitis: Inflammation of the testicles.

Otitis: Inflammation of the ear.

Otorrhoea: A purulent discharge from the ear.

Ovaritis: Inflammation of the ovaries.

Paralysis: A disease in which there is loss of power of voluntary movement in any part of the body.

Pectoral: A drug to cure disorders of the chest.

Pharyngitis: Inflammation of the pharynx.

Phythisis: Consumption; tuberculosis of the lungs.

Piles: An inflamed condition of the veins in the rectal region.

Pityriasis: A scaly skin disease.

Pleurisy: Inflammation of the membrane enclosing the lungs.

Pneumonia: Inflammation of the lungs.

Prolapse: The falling downward of an organ of the body from its normal position.

Prophylactic: An agent that prevents disease.

Prurigo: A chronic skin disease marked by the eruption of small, rounded, reddish pimples.

Psoriasis: A common chronic inflammation of the skin, marked by rounded reddened patches which are covered with dry silvery scales.

Puerperium: The period between childbirth and the return of the womb to its normal condition.

Pulmonary: Pertaining to the lungs.

Pyorrhoea: A disease marked by purulent discharge from the gums.

Refrigerant: A drug which relieves feverishness or produces a feeling of coolness.

Remittent fever: Fever in which the temperature fluctuates considerably, but does not drop to the normal.

Rheumatism: An indefinite term used for pains in the muscles, joints and certain tissues.

Ringworm: A parasitic skin disease usually marked by red, scaly, circular patches.

Roundworm: A pinkish, intestinal, parasitic worm resembling the common earthworm.

Rubefacient: A mild counter-irritant.

Scabies: An itching skin disease caused by a mite.

Sciatica: An inflammation of the sciatic nerve at the back of the thigh.

Scorbutic: Suffering from scurvy.

Scrofula: A disease of the lymphatic gland, often of the neck.

Scurvy: A deficiency disease due to lack of vitamin C.

Sedative: A drug which promotes salivation.

Sinus: Medically the term means a suppurating tract that has not healed up.

Soporific: A drug that induces sleep.

Sprue: Chronic inflammation of the digestive tract, marked by indigestion and morning diarrhoea.

Stomatitis: Inflammation of the mouth.

Strangury: Painful and drop by drop discharge of urine.

Stomachic: A drug that strengthens the stomach and promotes its action.

Styptic: An agent which checks bleeding.

Syphilis: A chronic venereal disease.

Tenesmus: Involuntary, painful, spasmodic and frequent straining to evacuate the bowel.

Tetanus: An infectious disease, marked by painful contraction in the muscles.

Threadworm: A very small thin worm commonly infecting children; its habitat is the large intestine.

Tonsilitis: Inflammation of the tonsils.

Tympanites: Distention of the abdomen due to the collection of gas.

Typhoid fever: An acute infectious disease characterized by ulceration of the intestines, eruption of rose-coloured spots, and a typical course of temperature.

Typhus fever: An acute contagious and infectious disease marked by high temperature, acute depression and eruptions.

Ulcer: An open sore on the skin.

Urethritis: Inflammation of the urethra, the canal which extends from the bladder and discharges the urine.

Urticaria: An allergic disease of systemic origin marked by painful and itching elevations of the skin.

Vermifuge: A drug which expels intestinal worms.

Vertigo: Dizziness.

Vesicant: An agent that produces a blister.

Vulnerary: A drug which promotes healing of wounds.

Wart: A hypertrophy of or growth on the skin.

Whipworm: A common parasite in men; the worm has a thick body and a slender neck; it resembles a whip.

Whitlow: A septic inflammation of the tissues surrounding the nail or of the bone of the distal joint of a finger or toe.

Whooping cough: An acute infectious disease characterized by peculiar spasmodic attacks of coughing.

Bibliography

1. Nadkarni, A.K., 1954, *Indian Materia Medica*, Bombay.
2. Kritikar, K.R. and B.D. Basu, 1935, *Indian Medicinal Plants*, Allahabad.
3. Chopra, I.C. and Nayyar S.L., 1956, *Glosssry of Indian Medicinal Plants*, New Delhi.
4. Dartin, J.F., 1951, *Medicinal Plants of India & Pakistan*, Bombay.
5. Jain, S.K., 1968, *Medicinal Plants*, New Delhi.
6. Chopra, R.N., 1958, *Chopra's Indigenous Drugs of India*, Calcutta.
7. Chopra, I.C. and Verma, B.S., 1969, *Supplement to Glossary of Indian Medicinal Plants*, New Delhi.
8. Huang, L., 1984, *Natural Products and Drug Research*, Munksgard, Copenhagen.
9. Suffness, M., 1995, *Taxol: Science and Application*, CRC Press.
10. Chiej, R., 1984, *Medicinal Plants*, Mac Donald, London.
11. Satyavati, G.V., Raina M.K. and Sharma M., 1976, *Medicinal Plants*, CSIR, New Delhi.
12. Wagner, H., 1981, *Natural Products as Medicinal Agents*, Hippocrats, Stuffgart.
13. Ambasta, P., 1987, *Useful Plants of India*, CSIR, New Delhi.
14. Kapoor, L.D., 1990, *Handbook of Ayurvedic Medicinal Plants*, CRC, Florida.
15. Dahanukar, S., 1995, *Heal with Herbs*, New Delhi.
16. Hameed, A, 1988, *A Complete Book on Home Remedies*, Orient Paperbacks, Delhi.
17. Dev, S., 1977, *Ethnotherapeutics and Modern Drug Development*, Curr. Sc., Bangalore.
18. Powell, F.W., 1973, *Health and Kitchen*, Health Science Press, England.
19. Mukerjee, K.R., 1983, *Protective Foods in Health and Disease*, Prakritik, Delhi.
20. Singh, S.J., 1982, *Food Remedies*, NCCMR, Lucknow.

Healing Power of FOODS

—Sunita Pant Bansal

Hippocrates, the father of medicine, stressed prevention of disease by strongly recommending a balanced diet with a moderate and sensible lifestyle.

This book introduces all the main food groups, details about the medicinal uses of the commonly used foods. The tips given are simple, practical and effective. The healthy recipes at the end of the book complete the role of the various foods in providing nutritional as well as medicinal benefits.

Demy Size • Pages: 136 • Price: Rs. 88/-

Kitchen Clinic

—Dr. Shiv Charan Sharma & Dr. Syed Aziz Ahmad

In this book, authors describe medicinal uses of 59 plants which are almost used in daily life in the kitchen of Indian homes. Botanical names, vernacular names, identification, distribution, medicinal uses have been given to each plant. In the middle of night or at odd hours when drug stores are closed, this book will give some alternate ways of controlling earaches, insomnia, minor burns, coughs, eczema, sore throats, etc.

Demy Size • Pages: 128 • Price: Rs. 80/-

Weight Loss—The Natural Way

—Dr. Rajeshwari

Today everyone is health and fitness conscious, regardless of age and sex. This book is aimed at those who would like to treat themselves naturally through the simple methods given. The aim of the book is to wean people away from harmful eating patterns and foods by giving them natural and healthy substitutes.

The book helps people to control obesity through: ❖ Yoga ❖ Acupuncture ❖ Acupressure ❖ Water Cure

Demy Size • Pages: 96 • Price: Rs. 80/-

Green Remedies

—Dr. S. Suresh Babu & Dr. M. Madhavi

This book chronicles about 80 green resources and over 600 simplified herbal recipes that are proven cures for a large number of frequently encountered ailments and common health problems. Indeed, green remedies are the most sought-after solutions for safe health management, preferred by all advanced Western nations. All medicinal recipes discussed are wholly based on sound ayurvedic medical texts.

Big Size • Pages: 244 • Price: Rs. 175/-

Postage: Rs. 15/- each. Every subsequent book: Rs. 5/-.

Nature Cure At Home

—Dr. Rajeshwari

Sometimes we resort to conventional methods for the most common and chronic disorders which can be easily overcome by simple natural methods without any side-effects.

The book is written for those readers who would like to take care of their own health, using simple remedies, exercises and dietary measures, without exposing themselves to the dangerous side-effects and reactions of potent drugs.

Demy Size • Pages: 232 • Price: Rs. 80/-

You are What you Eat

—Tanushree Podder

Did you know that food could heal, cure, elevate moods, improve memory, make the brain sharper, provide us with potent energy and fill us with vigour?

Food has been discovered to be the greatest natural pharmacy that is available to human beings. The right food can help us perform to our peak capacity while the wrong food can lead us towards disease and ill health. Use food for other benefits rather than just appeasing hunger.

Demy Size • Pages: 184 • Price: Rs. 96/-

The Joy of Natural Living

—Luis S.R. Vas & Anita S.R. Vas

This book incorporates research findings on health, psychology, body care and spirituality which emphasise the benefits of natural living. The more you rely on nature and nature therapy in dealing with your physical and mental problems, the more joy you get out of life.

Demy Size • Pages: 152 • Price: Rs. 96/-

Yoga for Health

—N.S. Ravi Shankar

Yoga today is universally acknowledged as a natural way to sound health and overall physical and mental well-being. And given its popularity, a variety of self-help yoga guides are available to the reader. But what makes this book unique is its approach and presentation. The book packs over 100 yogic asanas thoroughly illustrated, and backed by well-designed techniques to perform specific exercise from the first step to the last with each explanation followed by the therapeutic advantages of that posture.

Big Size • Pages: 184 • Price: Rs. 150/-

Postage: Rs. 15/- each. Every subsequent book: Rs. 5/-.